# CITIZEN ARIANNA

## THE HUFFINGTON POST / AOL MERGER: TRIUMPH OR TRAGEDY?

NANCY SNOW, PH.D

NIMBLE BOOKS LLC

NIMBLE BOOKS LLC

Nimble Books LLC

1521 Martha Avenue

Ann Arbor, MI, USA 48103

http://www.NimbleBooks.com

wfz@nimblebooks.com

+1.734-330-2593

Version 1.0; last saved 2011-07-19.

Printed in the United States of America

ISBN-13: 978-1-60888-116-1

The paper used in this publication meets the minimum requirements of the American National Standard for Information Sciences—Permanence of Paper for Printed Library Materials, ANSI Z39.48-1992. The paper is acid-free and lignin-free.

# DEDICATION

*For my mother, Suzanne Snow.*

NIMBLE BOOKS LLC

# CONTENTS

NIMBLE BOOKS LLC

# PRELUDE TO A STORM IN THE BLOGOSPHERE

The HuffPost-AOL merger is very personal for me, not only as a four-year blogger on *The Huffington Post*, but also as one who knows the main protagonist in this media marriage. Arianna Huffington is one of the most remarkable women I know, supremely canny and intelligent, über charming, with the gift of making you feel like you are the only one in the room with her—just like Bill Clinton can do—even though you really know better. Ironically I have pictures of myself with these charming bookends, Clinton in 1995 at the funeral of Senator J. William Fulbright, and Arianna as recently as 2009 when I was invited by Dean Lorraine Branham of the S.I. Newhouse School to attend the Mirror Awards, which that year was honoring Arianna.

Arianna is a people collector. I was once part of her temporary collection, though I knew I wouldn't make it to the permanent shelf because I'm not a typical person of influence. I'm a middle class gal from the Deep South, not famous, not rich, not LA, New York, or London; more like Birmingham, Richmond, and Florence (South Carolina!) I did hold a certain cachet in her collection as a college professor and head of Common Cause in New Hampshire, which was how we were first brought together. John McCain figures prominently in this story too, the 2000 version, not the 2008. I remember calling Arianna after McCain's loss to Bush in the South Carolina presidential primary. McCain had just won in New Hampshire "big time," to paraphrase G.W., but was killed off by a shoot-the-messenger campaign in the Palmetto state. As an eyewitness to the slaughter, I vowed that I would never live in South Carolina again; so far, that's a half-promise, as I have family there and visit regularly.

As I share in this short book, I had an adventure with Arianna at one point in my life. Now I watch her from afar. In spring and summer 2000, I was spending quite a bit of time at Arianna's Brentwood home. I had just moved to Los Angeles from the "Only Henniker on Earth" New Hampshire, and found myself caught in the web of the Greek media goddess. She wasn't the Queen of All Social Media back then. She was headlining the Shadow Conventions, what in hindsight were the stage versions of a blogging community. The Shadow Conventions consisted of her best celebrity friends and experts in their respective fields who served up their wisdom and wit in a Chautauqua-like backdrop to the insanity known as the real political conventions, the Democratic National Convention in LA and the Republican National Convention in Philadelphia.

I recall taking a ride with Arianna in a chauffeured Lincoln Town Car as we scouted Patriotic Hall in downtown Los Angeles. It would serve as the Shadow Convention headquarters for the Democratic National Convention. Anytime I was in the company of Arianna, I was akin to the Dos Equis commercial, the "Second Most Interesting Woman in the World." People were drawn to talking with me simply because I was with Arianna. A potted plant in Arianna's hand might have found a conversational partner. I've never had such a heady experience before or since, which included a rainy night limo ride to watch Arianna appear on HBO's "Dennis Miller Live" and another ride to watch Arianna work her magic on her good friend Bill Maher's late-night show, "Politically Incorrect." During this time Arianna would regularly invite me over to come to her home for some intimate dinner or salon that featured a prominent author or politician like Jesse Jackson, Arthur Schlesinger, or Norman Mailer. It was no big deal to open Arianna's front door to see Warren Beatty, Shirley MacLaine, Ed Asner, Larry King, Geraldo, pollster Pat Caddell or Donald Trump's ex-wife, Marla Maples, the latter with whom I shared our Georgia Peach connection. All of this socializing slowed down for me considerably after Arianna lost her mother in August 2000. I was never as connected to Arianna as I was becoming connected to her mother, Elli.

In this book my goal is to shine a little light on a person who is figuring so prominently in today's new media landscape. With Murdoch's kingdom in shambles post-*News of the World*, Arianna is flying higher than ever. It will be left up to you, dear reader, to decide if she is getting a little too close to the sun.

Nancy Snow, Ph.D.

# HEROINE OR HEEL?

"Some called him a hero, others called him a heel."

*Promo blurb about Charles Foster Kane*

2011 marks the 70th anniversary of *Citizen Kane*. The venerable *New York Times* gushed in 1941 that the film starring and directed by the boy genius Orson Welles was "one of the great (if not the greatest) motion pictures of all time."[1] *Citizen Kane* tells the story of Charles Foster Kane, a media mogul who answers to no one: "There is only one person in the world who's going to decide what I'm going to do and that's me." He's a citizen hero to those who see him take on fat cats on the front pages of his newspapers, and a ruthless heel to those who watch as he breaks all rules to fulfill his unquenching ambition for power. Kane has it all: he's confident, funny, energetic, unpredictable, and never boring. But in the end he dies a broken spirit, alone and without love, uttering the enigmatic "Rosebud," a word whose meaning the audience is left to ponder. It is a word for longing, something that the younger Kane desired and lost as a young boy.

Fast forward from 1941 to 2011 and witness that same *New York Times*, this time in the personage of its executive editor, Bill Keller, who is commenting on Citizen Arianna. There's no film version yet of one Arianna Stassinopoulos Huffington, the founder of the eponymous *Huffington Post*, but stay tuned. Keller has just announced that he's leaving the Times in September but before he goes, he directs a parting shot at the new media mogul, who from

1

her new perch at AOL has been poaching some of the best and brightest from his institution: "She is writing some big checks and it's pretty damned annoying. She's hired some good people."[2] These same words could have been said about Charles Foster Kane or his inspiration, William Randolph Hearst, equally famous for cherry picking the best people from Joseph Pulitzer's New York World to write for The New York Journal. It was as damned annoying then to Pulitzer as it is to Keller today. Keller had first tried to skewer his nemesis in a deeply personal diatribe against Huffington, the new face--not of L'Oréal--but of aggregation:

> "Aggregation" ... too often ... amounts to taking words written by other people, packaging them on your own Web site and harvesting revenue that might otherwise be directed to the originators of the material. In Somalia this would be called piracy. In the mediasphere, it is a respected business model.[3]

His departure in September could be seen as a peacef capitulation to the queen of online media. So why the venomous tone from one successful media executive to another? It all begins with one memorandum and the subsequent clicking and clacking 'round the blogosphere.

FADE IN:

MANHATTAN -- AOL HQ - 12:01 AM (9:01 PM PACIFIC)

ONE MINUTE AFTER SUPER BOWL SUNDAY, FEBRUARY 7, 2011

A memo is released to The Huffington Post community. It comes from Arianna Huffington, the co-founder and editor-in-chief of The Huffington Post. It is a spirited memo, full of anticipation and excitement. Primarily hers. The axe is about to fall on the neck of independent media..

The headline reads as follows:

## When HuffPost Met AOL: "A Merger of Visions"

It may be significant that the title echoed *When Harry Met Sally*, for Arianna was not given to revealing much about herself. In this press release, Arianna was letting her readers in on a very personal revelation: she was letting them know where her company was headed. The truth was there for all to see.

; Most of her readers, many of whom vehemently reject the corporatization and homogenization of news, wouldn't have imagined a corporate takeover of The Huffington Post, especially to AOL, a much maligned corporate media brand of the 1980s and 1990s. The Huffington Post was the most successful left-leaning Internet newspaper in the world. Surely, they believed, Arianna knew that and would protect its integrity. The news had to be broken somewhat gently to her soon-to-be-bereaved inamoratas so she carefully waited for several paragraphs before mentioning "the other man": AOL CEO Tim Armstrong.

> When Kenny Lerer and I launched The Huffington Post on May 9, 2005, we would have been hard-pressed to imagine this moment. The Huffington Post has already been growing at a prodigious rate. But my New Year's resolution for 2011 was to take HuffPost to the next level -- not just incrementally, but exponentially.
>
> At the first meeting of our senior team this year, I laid out the five areas on which I wanted us to double down: major expansion of local sections; the launch of international Huffington Post sections (beginning with HuffPost Brazil); more emphasis on the growing importance of service and giving back in our lives; much more original video; and additional sections that would fill in some of the gaps in what we are offering our read-

3

ers, including cars, music, games, and underserved minority communities.

Around the same time, I got an email from Tim Armstrong (AOL Chairman and CEO), saying he had something he wanted to discuss with me, and asking when we could meet.

The crux of the memo was that when Arianna met Tim, they were in synch, especially in their vision of their future bank accounts dancing like sugar plums in their heads[4] The old public image of The Huffington Post as a left-leaning rag be damned. The newly reconstituted HuffPost had the world at its fingertips, and if it lost its old readers to the AOL merger, millions of other readers stood on the sidelines waiting to climb on board the H express.

Over 7,000 HuffPost readers weighed in on the announcement, many in utter shock at this "merger of visions." They cut to the chase. Abandon HuffPost. Check out DemocracyNow.org, The Daily Kos, TruthDig, Alternet, any truly non-corporate media with a leftist edge. These sites weren't six-year "posers" like Huff-Post. They didn't play with people's feelings of community, of being part of something outside the corporate and conservative flag-waving mainstream. Some comments took action:

Trouble1971: I think it's time to take Huffpo out of my favorites. So disappointed.

Others used the occasion not just to vent their feelings, but to articulate a teachable moment:

Brettrobbins: One owner, seventy paid employees, hundreds of unpaid bloggers, millions of responders to what the bloggers write: guess who generates nearly all the revenue for this site? Guess who has absolutely no say in the direction in which the site goes, and who are expected to continue visiting it as frequently as they used to, despite the toxic AOL brand suddenly foisted upon them ?

I feel used

Nutcase (with 598 fans) wrote:

> Media conglomeration is the problem, not a solution. 85% of all books are published by 6 companies: 2 American, 2 British, 2 German. Each publisher is a minor component of a major corporation. They are told the limited amount they can spend on marketing. All of that goes to King, Gresham and others who don't need it. Comcast owns NBC. Disney owns ABC. Rupert owns Fox. Who cares who owns CBS?

> We cherished HuffPo because it was an independent progressive outlet. It is no longer independent. With 24/7 coverage of every breath taken by Sarah and Michelle, it has begun looking less progressive and much more TMZ.

> Say it isn't so, Joe.

The HuffPost-AOL merger was very personal for me, not only as a four-year blogger on The Huffington Post, but also as one who knew the main protagonist. I had first met Arianna Huffington a little over a decade earlier at a much different point in American media history when blogs weren't even in the lexicon. There was no Facebook, YouTube, Twitter, or social media discussion. We were a long way from an Arab Spring or Twitter Revolution in Iran.

In the late 90s and early 2000s, writing a syndicated op-ed column was still very much the norm, which is how I was first made aware of Arianna, along with her many television appearances on shows such as Bill Maher's "Politically Incorrect" and MSNBC's "Dennis Miller Live." As I read the comments aboutthe AOL acquisition, I began to think about a joke Arianna Huffington often told around the time of the 2000 presidential campaign. She spoke about the sorry state of money in politics and how expensive running for president had become. It was so bad that she pictured a time in America where just one voter named Bob living in Florida would be voting for George Bush, the XII, or some descendant of G.W. and G.H.W. Bush. I'd heard her tell the story several times and it was always one to get a laugh. It seemed so extreme, like a scene from a Tim Burton movie, a dark shadow on the American Realpolitik. Yes, we know that politics is dirty, but the press is a sacred sanctuary for the search for truth, right? Right?

It makes me think that someday every journalist will end up working for the Huffington Post Media Group, the Disneyland (something for everyone) of American journalism. This joke doesn't make me laugh.

# A BRAND NEW MEDIA UNIVERSE

I've told Tim I want to stay here forever. I want this to be the last act of my life.

—*Arianna Huffington, on uniting HuffPost with AOL*

She had the manners of an ambassador and the morals of a pirate.

—*Celeste Holm on fictional character Eve Harrington*

On Sunday, February 6, 2011, the underdog Green Bay Packers won Super Bowl XLV. Green Bay beat the favored Pittsburgh Steelers, a team whose quarterback Ben Roethlisberger had led to victory for two out of the last five world championships. In search of his third gold ring, he came up short.

Green Bay, Wisconsin is home to just over 100,000 people, a smaller number than the 110,000 capacity, at least those who could find their seats, at Cowboys Stadium in Arlington, Texas.[5] Cheesehead fans desperately needed a win to get over Bretichosis and Favreritis. With the victory, "Bret who?" of the Packers replaced last year's "Who dat?" of the New Orleans Saints.

The world seemed to be back in balance and proper alignment as the golden boy from the Golden State, Aaron Rodgers, beat the bad boy, Big Ben. Roethlisberger's off-field sexual abuses had led to his suspension from the first four games of the 2010 NFL season for violating the NFL's personal conduct policy, a policy that some members of the public were surprised even existed.

The Super Bowl festivities did not start out without a glitch. Back-to-back singing divas Lea Michele and Christina Aguilera sang "America the Beautiful" and the "Star-Spangled Banner" respectively, with Michele of the hugely popular TV show "Glee" getting the best of the five-time Grammy winner known as Xtina to her fans. Michele smiled and waved to the crowd and left the stage without incident. Aguilera, who seemed to want to outdo her upstart TV rival, chose to recreate her forgettable *Burlesque* movie performance with an emphasis on lengthy warbling instead of on knowing the lyrics. It should not take nearly two minutes to sing a mangled recreation of our national anthem.

While the actual football game had its exciting moments and Rodgers was named Most Valuable Player, it was merely a prelude to a major announcement that would cause many to forget just how badly Xtina sang or how many turnovers cost the Steelers the game. Super Bowl XLV, that über-American entertainment spectacle with its 111 million viewership, was upstaged for the cognoscenti by an even bigger spectacle. The Super Bowl was chosen as the backdrop for one of the most stunning media deals in this century.

In the Texas football crowd, obviously feeling like the Cheshire Cat, was none other than a born-again liberal media mogul hailing from Athens, Greece via London, New York, Washington, and Los Angeles. This cat has had as many lives and social identities as those cats in The Acropolis. Long before she was associated with online media, Arianna Huffington went through as many costume changes as Lady Gaga goes through meat purses and horns. The former darling of the political right in America when Newt Gingrich was dominating the Congressional chatter, the ex-wife of a conservative representative of Santa Barbara who later came out of the closet, the ex-Democratic gubernatorial candidate for governor of California in 2003, the Prius-loving populist whom the *Los Angeles Times* reported failed to pay taxes, was about to announce her last act.

As the game began, the sixty-year-old co-founder of the liberal online portal Huffington Post sat in anticipation in a corporate suite at Super Bowl XLV with the considerably younger CEO of AOL, the global media company formerly known as America Online. They were sitting on an announcement that would shock and rock the political continuum from left-leaning citizen activists and anti-war liberals who relied on the Huffington Post for comfort and commentary to the follow-the-leader, socially conservative Middle Americans and seniors who had signed up with  dinosaur AOL in its glory days when dial-up was king.

By the time of the halftime show of the Super Bowl, when Fergie and the Black Eyed Peas were making us all wish for younger days, Arianna Huffington and Tim Armstrong were jetting off to New York to get ready for the media blitz that would require their presence on virtually every network imaginable. In a 24-hour media blitzkrieg reminiscent of Orwell's *1984*, there sat the eternally gorgeously coiffed and very fit-looking Huffington belying her age in her trendy dress pantsuit, with her besuited and besotted suitor beside her, AOL executive Tim Armstrong.

After the year of the tiger and in the year of the rabbit, the cougar was center stage, with progressives scattering in panic like so many hares.

# AOL: Really?! AOL: Really!

Outside the media insider and tech worlds, Tim Armstrong was a relatively obscure former Google executive who had joined AOL in 2009. As head of a company known more for its media busts than its media brilliance contemplated an alliance with a modern day Citizen Kane, one could feel the nearly breathless sense of excitement emanating from Armstrong. He was joining forces with the one-word brand known as Arianna.

By the same token, one could see the dollar signs replacing the pupils in the eyes of Arianna Huffington, as she expected to cash a 10% payday check from the $315 million buyout. The faltering AOL and the trendy Huffington Post ("the HuffPo") had merged visions and property to create what they called a brand new media universe.

As I watched the interminable whirlwind of sit-down publicity that battered media fans like a hurricane for days after the announcement, a bold pattern of authoritarian clichés and subconscious memes emerged:

> **CONTENT IS KING**
> **1+1=11**
> **SYNERGY**
> **WOMEN BUY, BUY WOMEN**
> **FEMALE ENTREPRENEUR**
> **MOVE OVER, OPRAH**
> **POLITICS IS DEAD**

To be fair, America Online (now strictly known as AOL) was once king of all online media, if being king means beating out has-been rivals like CompuServe and Prodigy. Its AOL software CDs were as omnipresent as Southern kudzu—and just as impossible to avoid—and its email audible "You've Got Mail" was once relevant enough that it was indelibly associated with Meg Ryan's 1990s-era face. From the mid 1990s until 2000, nothing could stop AOL as the largest online service provider in the world, which is what probably led to its hubristic notion (aka boneheaded idea) that it could be king of the media universe.

Long before Facebook, Apple's iTunes, and Twitter, the younger and hipper media homecoming queens and kings that erased AOL's dominance and everything else in their path, AOL was the coolest web portal in the dot com universe. In 2000, the Internet colossus shocked the media world when it announced its engagement to the traditional media global titan Time Warner in a lavish ceremony for $164 billion. In 2001, the two companies officially tied the knot. And with this ISP I now thee wed, a new media universe was born: AOL Time Warner. But the marriage of the new media with the old media was like two monotheistic religions clashing in Samuel Huntington's "clash of civilizations." The hoped-for wedded bliss faltered and fizzled when the merger was promptly followed by the burst of the first Internet bubble eventually leading to a $99 billion financial bath that left many bodies strewn in its path.

Three of the walking dead to depart the media marriage were one-time TBS and CNN media mogul Ted Turner, CEO of Time Warner Gerald Levin, and America Online boy wonder Steve Case, but their losses were still gains in comparison to the losses suffered by the masses in the name of convergence. Easily forgotten in the boardroom bloodletting were thousands of nameless and faceless workaday employees who were fired to make the company a lean, mean, new media machine.

By 2003 AOL Time Warner stopped using its married name as lawsuits, departures, and most notably, the company's value continued to bleed. In 2006, AOL's Internet customer base had dropped by over one-third to under 19 million from its high of 30 million. It had little relevance in an online marketplace of ideas now dominated by that funny-sounding search engine company known as Google. In an effort to remain marginally relevant, AOL dropped its mandatory paid subscriber model like an old Members Only™ jacket and declared that its service and email were now free to all comers, so long as you didn't mind constant advertising traffic (remember the kudzu). AOL's partnership with Time Warner officially split in 2009. As of 2011, AOL was still making 80% of its revenue from paid subscribers who either most likely didn't know or less likely didn't care that anyone could access for free AOL's content, including its email service, at AOL dot com.

# THE MORNING-AFTER PILL

Occasionally people come together, sexually or otherwise, and regret it the next day. And such is the case of companies too. If one were to judge the post-Super Bowl AOL-Huffington Post announcement by public reaction alone, you might think that this was a dinner date best kept private. But since this announcement was essentially a merging of brands, one tarnished, the other golden, it required a reveal that would make P.T. Barnum envious.

Both Arianna Huffington and her namesake virtual self extension, were perceived for six years (2005-2011) as an independent liberal/left answer to Matt Drudge and the Drudge Report, Rupert Murdoch's Fox News Channel, and the conservative talk radio/TV blathering of Rush Limbaugh, Glenn Beck and Sean Hannity. Without Arianna as the "face" of the Huffington Post, the site would very likely have faltered. It struggled after a few fits and starts, such as the time in March 2006 when George Clooney was not happy about his byline appearing on a Huffington Post page. He was not a HuffPost blogger and, as it turned out, his comments from two interviews, one with Larry King and the other with the *Guardian* newspaper in London, were simply reposted at HuffPost without explanation of their origin.[6] Arianna explained the process:

> When I first invited George Clooney to blog after a screening of Good Night, and Good Luck a few months ago, he said he wasn't sure how a blog worked. So we put together a sample blog from answers he had given on Larry King Live and an interview with the Guardian in London, and sent it to him to rework in any way he wanted.

A publicist who was working on the promotion of Good Night, and Good Luck, emailed back saying, "I will get it to him and get back to you as soon as I hear anything." Three days later, she emailed again, approving, without any changes, what we had sent: "Of course this is fine, Arianna!"

And once we had the approval, that's what we ran: George Clooney's words put into blog form.

This was an honest misunderstanding. But any misunderstanding that occurred, occurred between Clooney and the publicist. We based our decision to post on the unambiguous approval we received in writing. There was no room for misunderstanding in that.

Clooney's response:

Miss Huffington's blog is purposefully misleading and I have asked her to clarify the facts. I stand by my statements but I did not write this blog. With my permission Miss Huffington compiled it from interviews with Larry King and The Guardian. What she most certainly did not get my permission to do is to combine only my answers in a blog that misleads the reader into thinking that I wrote this piece. These are not my writings -- they are answers to questions and there is a huge difference.

Despite Clooneygate, and after a very successful time covering the rise of candidate and then new president Barack Obama, by 2010 Arianna had built her site into a SEO (search engine optimization) extraordinaire with an army of some 6,000 volunteer bloggers who could vanity publish whilst their work sat side-by-side salacious entertainment and clunky and chewy celebrity nuggets. The Huffington Post turned profitable that year for the first time, bringing in advertising revenue of approximately $31 million, which explains AOL's valuing the company generally, and in particular, Ms. Huffington, at ten times revenue in February 2011.

Very little of the HuffPost content was ever original independent journalism, which was probably not Huffington's goal from the start. Arianna Huffington had been utilizing the Internet for over a decade and had a popular website promoting her ideas called Arianna Online, eerily similar sounding to the AOL she rules today. Huffington's plan was to create a Huffington Internet marketing brand with a big H branding logo. Her popular following among liberals and leftists was really a side dish, not a main course, to her Huffington Post operation. Some of her bloggers were the famous liberal-left glitterati: Warren Beatty, Nora Ephron, Deepak Chopra, Oliver Stone, Arthur Schlesinger, Norman Mailer, Gwyneth Paltrow, even Barack Obama. (He doesn't blog as president of the United States.) Most of her bloggers were not famous but were more than happy to be appearing as extras in the media extravaganza with the trademarked H. Once the AOL takeover was announced, it was quite transparent to the majority of onlookers that Huffington's motivations—with Armstrong's blessings of course-- were for enlarging her personal brand (from earth to far-away galaxies), and, by extension, her newly acquired media content at AOL. Armstrong and AOL clearly were on the short end of this stick, both financially and brand-wise. AOL acknowledged the Huffington Media Empire by announcing that Arianna Huffington would be editor-in-chief of all AOL content properties in a newly formed Huffington Post Media Group.

In the post-merger rea, the Huffington Post still looks quite the same, perhaps to slowly warm the water to the boiling point for all those frogs. The majority of original content at the Huffington Post still centers around the free content from the bloggers' opinion pieces, but obviously the value in HuffPo is not staked on this platform of bloggers, many of whom are friends and acquaintances of Huffington. (Writer/director Nora Ephron, a longtime friend of Huffington's from her New York days, was the first woman Arianna asked to blog for the Huffington Post. She is listed as HuffPo's editor at large.)

No, the value of HuffPo lies in the fact that to date no other web community is as savvy as the Huffington Post in making its stories "sticky," that is, replied to, forwarded, re-tweeted, and re-posted. A worker bee population of very young staff is used to troll the Internet for what is trending, be it Lindsay Lohan's sticky fingers or Egypt's Tahrir Square protests. The formula is, like the magazine, real simple: cut-and-paste stories are branded with the Huffington Post logo online at a dizzying rate no competitor can match. And who wants to compete with the Huffington Post, anyway? Media observer Tim Rutten of the *Los Angeles Times* explains the Huffington Post routine in the most unflattering light imaginable:

> The bulk of the site's content is provided by commentators, who work for nothing other than the opportunity to champion causes or ideas to which they're devoted. Most of the rest of the content is "aggregated"—which is to say stolen—from the newspapers and television networks that pay journalists to gather and edit the news.
>
> The Huffington Post is a brilliantly packaged product with a particular flair for addressing the cultural and entertainment tastes of its overwhelmingly liberal audience. To grasp its business model, though, you need to picture a galley rowed by slaves and commanded by pirates. Given the fact that its founder, Huffington, reportedly will walk away from this acquisition with a personal profit of as much as $100 million, it makes all the Post's raging against Wall Street plutocrats, crony capitalism and the Bush and Obama administrations' insensitivities to the middle class and the unemployed a bit much.
>
> The fact is that AOL and the Huffington Post simply recapitulate in the new media many of the worst abuses of the old economy's industrial capitalism—the sweatshop, the speedup and piecework; huge profits for the owners; desperation, drud-

gery and exploitation for the workers. No child labor, yet, but if there were more page views in it ...

The Super Bowl Surprise was a stake in the heart of liberal netizens (and political independents) who felt taken, had, betrayed, bamboozled, deceived—anything but celebratory—about the merger. The collective sentiment was that Citizen Arianna was selling out her soul to an online company with a terrible track record in mergers and acquisitions.

# HER DANCE PARTNER: THEY SHOOT COMPANIES, DON'T THEY?

After the media debacle of the first decade of the 21st Century with Time Warner, AOL, spinster-like, spurned other lovers. It overvalued companies like the Israel technology company Mirabilis, developer of the instant messenger service ICQ, which it bought for over $407 million in June 1998 and sold for $187.5 million in June 2009 and Bebo, a social networking site that AOL bought for $850 million in March 2008 and sold for $10 million in June 2010. Tim Armstrong said that the Bebo firesale would create a "meaningful tax deduction," apparently blissfully ignorant of the Wall Street Journal's description that the AOL Bebo sale was, like an Arnold Schwarzenegger thriller, a total value destruction. So far be it for the eternally optimistic Arianna Huffington to downplay a second-decade AOL acquisition of her company. Instead, she referred to the AOL-HuffPo event as a "Sputnik Moment." On February 7, 2011, she released a statement to the Huffington Post community with Champagne delusion and Super Bowl dazzle still buzzing in her head. She even used new math, or at least the kind one might use at a Ramada Inn wedding reception: "1 + 1 = 11."

Describing her lunch meeting with Tim Armstrong in January 2011, just one month before the deal was announced, she gushed, "I laid out my vision for the expansion of The Huffington Post, and he laid out his vision for AOL. We were practically finishing each other's sentences." Tim Armstrong, who once headed ad sales at Google, had jumped on board the sinking AOL ship in 2009, albeit with the best of motivations: he received $25.5 million in compensation for 2009.[7] Besides the Bebo sale, Armstrong was also known for presiding over, what else, a logo change at AOL. For decades the company was known through its triangle identity but on December 10, 2009 a new logo was launched with AOL adopting a large cap A followed by lower cap o and l with a period after the name. The date marked a dramatic change in AOL's status: it was once again independent forever from Time Warner and would now trade on the New York Stock Exchange. The new logo is stamped over rotating feel-good images (peace sign, goldfish), like a poor man's Google Doodle.

Leaving aside the possibility of romance or the clash of overbearing personalities, there is a good explanation for why Arianna and Tim were completing each other's sentences. Armstrong has spent his entire career in marketing and sales, and Arianna is a natural marketer and saleswoman. He and Arianna quickly found a common fertile ground—commercial propaganda—from which to expand their AOL and Huffington brands. For we huddling masses who sit eating our movie popcorn and clapping when prompted, Arianna Huffington promised this: "Far from changing our editorial approach, our culture, or our mission, this moment will be for HuffPost like stepping off a fast-moving train and onto a supersonic jet." (Presumably, without falling in the gap between.) :We're still traveling toward the same destination, with the same people at the wheel, and with the same goals, but we're now going to get there much, much faster." One can hear Billy Joel singing "Just the Way You Are" in the background.

Within hours of the announcement, Arianna Huffington was hitting all the right notes to sound like a supersonic corporate jet.

Huffington and Armstrong told Sharon Waxman, editor of The Wrap Dot Com, that they received thousands of emails from well-wishers whose typical greeting began with "Wow!" Added Armstrong: "Almost ever yemail we got from every influential person basically started with that. And I think the second words were 'very smart.'" (Apparently Armstrong had never heard of the ancient royal practice of diplomatic flattery.) Armstrong glowed that Arianna Huffington got a standing ovation from AOL employees when she was introduced, as if the alternative were a Bronx cheer. (That Bronx cheer might have been in order on March 4th when AOL announced it was shedding 900 jobs.) The AOL CEO couldn't stop himself from trafficking meme coinages such as "best news and information female entrepreneur" who "commands the women's space on the web." .

When asked by Waxman if AOL would become left leaning or progressive in its content, Arianna smiled and said, with ice-crystal clarity, "People forget that the Huffington Post consists of twenty-six sections and only fifteen percent of our traffic comes from politics." Huffington told Waxman that the Huffington Post as absorbed by AOL would experience political shrinkage: "AOL is not a political site. AOL has Politics Daily, a section which covers politics, but it's not a political site. I was always clear that HuffPo would not just be a political site. I always wanted it to be an Internet newspaper, covering every aspect of life."[8]

# ALL ABOUT ARIANNA (FOR THE UNINITIATED)

The most fascinating, newsworthy aspect to the AOL-HuffPost deal beyond the headline grabbing multimillions is Arianna Huffington herself. Were she not at the helm of her Internet newspaper Huffington Post, the deal with AOL would have been far less controversial, even a yawn. It is who she is—or at least who she presents herself to be—that makes all the difference. And what makes her tick deep down is as enigmatic as any fictional Hollywood character like Charles Foster Kane or Eve Harrington. There are certain people who come along whose background and presence are so unique that they cannot be ignored. Arianna Huffington is, like Eve Harrington, a most unforgettable character. She is, like Eve, often not well liked for her ambition and aggressive pursuit of stardom. She was famously called by the Guardian's Michael White "the most upwardly mobile Greek since Icarus."[9] Anyone who comes into Arianna's orbit--and she is, like the planets and the stars, constantly in motion—will have a chance to sip from the cup of her formidable influence. And what is more powerful in America than politics, media, and celebrity?. They are the troika of money and power in America. If one can conquer all three, or at least two out of three, you win, at least until you die.

Arianna failed at politics, but she is on the verge of a media kingdom the likes of which we haven't seen Katharine "The Great" Graham ruled Washington. As amNewYork called it, "Arianna Huffington: The Making of a Mogul." Writer Emily Ngo referred to Arianna in language fit for a Hollywood marquee (or a headline in *Variety*): "maven," "queen," "glamazon."[10]

Born in Athens, Greece on July 15, 1950, Arianna's dream was to study at Cambridge University in England. After her mother, Elli Stassinopoulos, separated from Arianna's father. she moved to England with Ariadne Anna (Arianna) and her younger sister Agapi Arianna's rise to fame began early when she became president of the world-famous Cambridge Union debating society. It didn't hurt that she was a 5'10" beauty who turned heads as quickly as her Eva Gabor-like accent broke hearts. (Arianna claims her height was a detriment as a young tween when she also suffered from acne, wore thick eyeglasses and had unmanageable curly hair.)

While at Cambridge, Arianna began a ten-year affair with Bernard Levin, her senior by twenty-two years, who was to be the most influential person in her life after her mother. Their "pillow talk" was her best liberal education, or so Levin told his young protégé, and she claims him as the big love of her life. Levin's career was a perfect model for Arianna's. Slight of build, he was a big media man. A prolific author and the most influential journalist of his day as a columnist with *The Times* of London, Levin held sway through the power of his pen and his regular appearances on television programs like *Good Evening*, *That Was the Week That Was*, and *Face the Music*. It was on the panel show *Face the Music* that Levin first met the redheaded bombshell Arianna Stassinopoulos and after their face-to-face they made their own sweet music. It was not Levin's braininess, however, but his commitment to lifelong bachelorhood that led Arianna to move to New York in 1980. Within a few years she conquered the Big Apple and married the most eligible bachelor (code for "filthy rich unmarried male") that the city had to offer in 1986—Michael Huffington, the reclusive Republican son of a Texas oil billionaire whose father worried would never marry. Marry he did, and in a very big way, to a woman who steals oxygen out of every room she enters. The twosome had daughters Christina and Isabella, and Michael had a one-term career as a Santa Barbara congressman during the Newt Gingrich era, what was then the most expensive congressional political campaign at $5.4 million. He and Arianna divorced in 1997 and Michael revealed a year later to David Brock in *Esquire* magazine that he was sexually attracted to men and had been his whole life.

# MEETING CITIZEN ARIANNA

Although Arianna Huffington's life revolves around two main locations, New York City and Los Angeles, it was along the byways of a tiny New England state of New Hampshire that I first met her. If you don't know about New Hampshire, its location is between Massachusetts and Vermont, also known as Taxachusetts and the People's Republic of Vermont to those politically right of center. Known for its fierce independence, the state motto, Live Free or Die displayed prominently on automotive licenses, New Hampshire's pride of place in the primary schedule enables it to occupy an enormously important position in presidential campaigns despite its bucolic, overwhelmingly rural, white, and affluent million plus population of only one million. Its demographics may not reflect the rest of the United States, but the New Hampshire Way in presidential politics is to kick the tires. New Hampshire voters see the same candidates over and over, just as Tammany Hall ward clerks used to see the same voters. The big states like California and New York are simply too big for this retail politics approach, where future White House occupants glad-hand voters at ice cream socials, in living rooms, and at mom and pop stores like the century-old Henniker Pharmacy in the heart of the Only Henniker on Earth, my college hometown for four and a half years.

In New Hampshire, presidential candidates know you by face and remember your name. I was on a first-name basis with several, including Paul Wellstone and John McCain, both of whom I hosted at New England College. I moderated presidential forums with Alan Keyes and Phil Gramm for New Hampshire Public Radio and met legendary also-rans Eugene McCarthy and George McGovern. My first foray into New Hampshire was in January 1992 to support the appearance of Democratic presidential candidate Jerry Brown who was speaking at New England College in Henniker. Brown succeeded twice in obtaining the one elective office that Arianna Huffington sought in 2003 and from which she quickly retreated, that of California governor. This political turn was the biggest blunder of her otherwise impressive run for greater influence and power.

For any political animal, living in the Granite State is a great career-starter. Not only is it possible for a seemingly unknown presidential candidate to gain national recognition as a result of doing well in New Hampshire, but for anyone who studies, teaches, and comments on politics, living in the state allows you a front-row seat to the action. Since the Eisenhower win in 1952, New Hampshire had seared its national reputation as the political genie forecaster. New Hampshire primary winners always predicted general election presidential winners until Bill Clinton ruined everything in 1992 by losing the primary to favorite son Paul Tsongas, and to the non-candidate, but equally influential, Gennifer Flowers. Two other New Hampshire surprises followed: John McCain's big victory over George W. Bush in 2000 and Hillary Clinton's comeback win over Barack Obama in 2008.

I met Arianna on January 30, 2000, but our initial connection was preceded by an email and phone call a few weeks earlier. Our meeting was probably not unlike thousands of others she has had over her adult lifetime in the public domain: a stranger contacting her for an interview. In my case, I was a book author and professor of political science at New England College, a liberal arts college which, because of its location in Henniker about 20 minutes out-

25

side the state capitol of Concord, was a convenient location for many presidential candidates to appear, including Jerry Brown in 1992. I also was acting as executive director and media spokesperson for Common Cause of New Hampshire, a nonpartisan good-government citizens' lobby that is the type of nonprofit lobby Arianna would likely champion. Common Cause was a prominent player in the presidential politics of Campaign 2000, most notably for its heavy lobbying on behalf of the McCain-Feingold campaign finance bill. The campaign finance efforts by Common Cause had the support of both Bill Bradley among Democratic presidential candidates and McCain among the Republicans. We may forget now just how significant campaign finance was as a political issue before September 11, 2001, but it had grown in prominence following a series of financial scandals in the Clinton White House including the the Lincoln Bedroom cash-for-crash pad program, White House "Coffees" for prominent DNC donors, Buddhist Temple fundraisers, and the infamous "Chinagate" when PRC representatives paid illegal foreign contributions to influence the outcome of the U.S. election.

Arianna was writing a nationally syndicated column that kept me guessing about her political persuasion. Her late 90s columns were moving gradually from right to left. (For an archive of her columns, including around the time of our meeting, see Arianna Online.)[11] I was curious about her political transformation from far right friend to Newt to more moderate populist and I wondered why so I emailed her an introduction and asked if I might interview her for a section on "Women of Vision" in *Washington International* magazine, a monthly based in the nation's capitol that caters to the diplomatic community and international traveler. I had no idea if she would respond, but I have often said that college professors are about as threatening as babies and kittens. Our motives seem pure, or at least less tainted since our entire career rests on credibility and reputation. Nevertheless it was a pleasant surprise to hear back from her given that I wasn't calling from *Time* or *Newsweek*. Arianna called and left a message on my answering machine that she was coming to New Hampshire for the presidential primary (there was no texting in those days of innocence)) I never did conduct that interview, but I got something better: the sound of Arianna's thick Greek accent on my answering machine in Henniker, which I have ever since loved to mimic. "Nancy, it's Arianna. I'm coming to New Hampshire. We'll have to meet." That was it. I was hooked. Years before the Huffington Post would net thousands of blogging fish--of which this little minnow would be one--I had heard from The Voice. My perspective on media, politics, power and persuasion, would forever be altered.

I was already familiar with the media version of Arianna Huffington through hair, voice, and bed.

In the 1990s she had Republican hair, the fashionable kind one recalls seeing on FOG (Friend of George) Georgette Mosbacher, who was married to the chairman of the U.S. Chamber of Commerce Robert Mosbacher.

Like Georgette, Arianna had that perfectly coiffed red flowing hair that signaled a personage of elegance and class who never, ever, ever missed an appointment with her personal stylist.

Arianna's voice was unmistakable. No one sounded like her, or at least no one since Zsa Zsa Gabor had starred in *Green Acres*.

Arianna's bed-in with Al Franken (he in his nightcap, she in her lingerie) for the "Strange Bedfellows" segment on ABC's "Politically Incorrect" with Bill Maher had left an indelible imprint on my memory

Each time I saw her she was smart, funny, and easy on the eyes, with a high Q Score for the visual medium. Her accent was incredibly sexy—no getting around that for anyone who has traveled to Greece and experienced it in surround-sound. The only trouble was that it was so thick that viewers often found her very hard to follow, which made her even less forgettable: I would ask people if they knew Arianna from television and often get a reply like this: "Oh, you mean that lady with the Greek accent whom I can't understand."

In 2000, Huffington, then a close friend to John McCain, was backing the Arizona senator over the Texas governor George W. Bush for the Republican presidential nomination. I met her at a Bill Bradley speech at Franklin Pierce Law School where Bradley supporter Cornel West was described by Arianna thusly: "He watched Bradley so intently it seemed he was trying to give him a passion transfusion."[12] We proceeded to meet up over several days, crossing the snowy foothills of New Hampshire in my 1998 Honda Civic, shadowing candidates from town hall to living room, and occasionally meeting with journalists aboard the Straight Talk Express McCain campaign bus. We went from a McCain rally for war veterans in Franklin to a prominent Republican donor's home in Hopkinton for Super Bowl party. This was followed by another stop at the Black Brimmer in Manchester at a Bill Bradley rally where she talked with Bill Bradley's other bookend supporter, Senator Bob Kerrey of Nebraska, and I fended off adoring fans who sought to be planets in her orbit. Arianna's January 31, 2000 column described the McCain momentum leading into the Tuesday primary:

I left McCain at a friend's home, surrounded by adoring supporters, many of them too young to vote, watching the Rams barely hold on to beat the Titans. I then went on to Bradley's Super Bowl bash at the Black Brimmer in Manchester, where the crowd went wild when Bradley was introduced by Sen. Bob Kerrey (D-Neb.) as "the most uncorruptible politician I've ever met."

Kerrey was followed by Cornel West, who urged the assembled to "send a message to America" about a new day of a New Politics. "I'm traveling with him," West had told me earlier in the day with a twinkle in his eye, "to make sure he stays connected with his soul."

It's a worthy endeavor, but those pesky Independents seem to have decided that although Bradley is talking a lot about a soulful New Politics, McCain is the one outraged enough about the old politics to lead the charge against it.

When she rode with me to gatherings, Arianna sat comfortably in the back seat of my compact car as she made or took one cell phone call after another. I'm hoping that this meant there was someone else with us, but I'm not sure if that were the case. The cell phone beside her ear was a constant presence, enough to serve as a third person. (This all came back to me when Arianna made national news in January 2011 for enraging a fellow airline passenger who saw her using a Blackberry during the FAA-regulated forbidden time at take-off.)[13]

On the Monday following the Sunday madness, I came over to her hotel room in Manchester where she received yet another phone call from some guy named Warren. "Warren, you should have been here," she said. TV repairman? No. It quickly dawned on me that she was talking to the actor and political activist Warren Beatty. Beatty's Senator Jay Bulworth film portrayal in 1998 had led some of the more liberal members of the Democratic Party to consider him a credible candidate to challenge the Republicans for the presidential nomination. Beatty himself felt dissatisfied with the narrow choices of either Vice President Gore or his presumptive challenger, Bill Bradley. Arianna had mounted an effort to get Beatty to jump into the fray through her syndicated columns and Brentwood salons but Beatty had publicly announced he would not seek the nomination. By February 2000, Arianna was clearly still sorry that Warren Beatty had not at least made a personal appearance at some of the New Hampshire town hall meetings and debates. I was too. As I sat at the edge of Arianna's bed as she conducted her business while poking a fork at her room service steak, I knew that Dorothy had once left Kansas and that Nancy would soon leave New Hampshire. Arianna was a tornado of access and influence and she had shown me a whole new world.

It was stunning to see Arianna work a crowd. I've never seen it before or since, but then I'm not one who is usually in the Hollywood Jet Set or at a political fundraiser at Oprah's home in Montecito, California. Everyone in little ole New Hampshire wanted a piece of Arianna Huffington. She was easy to spot in a crowdhad the gift of grab and gab.. She would grab someone, gab a little, and then that person would just keep following her. I know because I was in her orbit enough to be constantly asked if so-and-so could have a minute with Ms. Huffington. I realized that my close proximity to Arianna had been mistaking for my being her publicist or assistant. It didn't bother me one bit and I played a game with the mistaken identity. I would tell the person, "Ms. Huffington is very busy, as you know. I'll see what I can do." Proximity breeds similarity. Just standing with her at a bar made otherwise indifferent famous people more than happy to meet me. I was Nancy Who, for sure, but if I were with Ms. Huffington then I was worthy of a handshake or hello. The stars were out in force: Jon Stewart, Chris

Matthews, Mike Myers of Clinton's White House, Andrea Mitchell of NBC News, Larry King, Tony Snow, Tom Brokaw. Anyone and everyone in politics and media were present in Manchester, New Hampshire in the days leading to February 1, 2000.

I was with Arianna the night that McCain beat Bush by an enormous unexpected margin of 19 percentage points. We were present at his victory speech, thrilled and excited about McCain's ability to use his "maverick" status to upset the status quo "son of Barbara" George W. Bush. The summer before I met Arianna I had already been stirring the pot on my own. When Bush came to New Hampshire—he was famously lacking in personal appearances whereas McCain had attended one hundred-plus town hall meetings—I took the opportunity to use my Common Cause position to stage a stunt. Since public opinion polls deemed campaign finance reform as one of the top priorities for Campaign 2000, I decided to dress as a pastry chef and appear at one of Governor Bush's Fourth of July campaign stops. He and his security entourage of Texas Rangers were stopping at a mom-and-pop ice cream stand in southern New Hampshire where Bush was—I'm not kidding here— serving "Compassionate Conservative Creamsicles." I arrived early to stake out my place on the public sidewalk. I had on my chef's pants (which I still have today), a chef's hat, and a big bowl of cookie dough with a large wooden spoon. On the bowl it read: "Recipe for a Presidency: Lots and Lots of Dough." I was a media sensation, albeit on a small scale, given that I was holding court on a sidewalk adjacent to Madden's Ice Cream and Food Stand in Merrimack, New Hampshire. But I managed to score interviews with the ABC News affiliate in Atlanta, Georgia as well as with a young cub reporter from the *Concord Monitor*, Aaron Bowden, son of *Black Hawk Down* writer Mark Bowden.[14]

# SPLITTING INFINITIES

With full awareness of the meaning of my words and the responsibility of what I am about to say, it is my considered belief that Mr. Charles Foster Kane, in every essence of his social beliefs and by the dangerous manner in which he has persistently attacked the American traditions of private property, initiative and opportunity for advancement, is—in fact—nothing more or less than a Communist.

*--Trustee Thatcher for Charles Foster Kane*

In *Citizen Kane*, Charles Foster Kane is a man of humble origins who rises to great wealth and influence after his parent's mine—a gift from a debt—is discovered full of gold. His parents elect to put young Kane in the care of a trustee, the New York banker Walter Parks Thatcher. Kane uses his family's wealth to buy a newspaper, the *New York Inquirer*, and promises to always tell the truth to his readers and uphold the highest standards of journalism. His principles don't match his behavior. He uses yellow journalism tactics to outsell his competition ("You provide the prose poems; I'll provide the war.") He acquires the best staff from his chief rival, the *Chronicle*, calling his new hires "collectibles." Kane's guardian Thatcher is troubled by the manner in which Charles Foster Kane champions newspaper campaigns that undermine Thatcher's business interests. After Kane uses his media platform to run unsuccessfully for governor of New York, Thatcher tells a Congressional committee that Kane is in fact a Communist and is not to be trusted by anyone. Throughout the film, Kane remains an enigma, and the viewer is left wondering what, if any, true convictions citizen Kane ever really had.

Like Kane, Arianna Huffington remains an enigma, even as she reaches what she has characterized as her "last act."

Arianna Huffington was born to a Greek publisher father, Constantine, who edited an underground National Resistance newspaper, *To Paron*, (The Present) during the Nazi occupation of Greece. His political activism and opposition journalism led to internment in the Nazi concentration camps Haidari in Athens and Neugammen and Beendorf in Germany. After the war he became General Secretary of the Ministry of Finance and edited *To Paron* in its postwar form as an aboveground weekly newspaper.

Arianna's mother, Elli Stassinopoulos, was also active in the Greek resistance against the Nazis. Fluent in German, Elli saved two Jewish girls from the Nazis by hiding with them in a cabin in the mountains and telling the German soldiers in their pursuit that their search was futile and they could put their guns away. Arianna mentions her mother in most any personal interview she gives. Elli, whom I got to know in the last few months before her death, had a completely different constitution from her daughter. Elli's rhythm was slow and contemplative. Her daughter Arianna's was fast and fleeting. When you sat with Elli, she concentrated completely on you. When you sat with Arianna, she concentrated on you for a few seconds until the phone rang or a problem needed resolving. It was emotionally soothing to be with Arianna's mother. I always felt like my blood pressure, which is already normal to below normal, was lowered around Elli. Whenever I left Elli, I thought to myself, what a gift to spend time with this fascinating matriarch of two daughters and two granddaughters.

Elli lived with Arianna for most of Arianna's life, and that is why Arianna still holds her mother as her greatest female influence.

Without Elli, it is hard to say if Arianna would have had the strength and backbone to rise to where she is today. Her mother was her greatest champion and her most honest critic. I'm not sure if Citizen Arianna has anyone today who can replace that honesty.

I recall sitting with Elli on the back patio at Arianna's Brentwood home, where Elli lived, and admiring the color of just one petal of a flower. Arianna was always in her office, often on the phone or talking to her staff upstairs. We would exchange waves with each other as I was walking by her first floor office to visit with Elli in her bedroom. Elli was like a Greek philosopher, one who doles out wisdom with a few choice words or phrases. I listened intently whenever I was with Elli, but never realized that our relationship would be so short. Arianna described her mother most recently for International Women's Day (March 8, 2011):

> Her life had the rhythm of a timeless world, a child's rhythm. In her world, there were no impersonal encounters -- it was a world where a trip to the farmer's market happily filled half a day, where there was always enough time for wonder at how lovely the rosemary looked next to the lavender. In fact, going through the market with her was like walking through the Louvre with an art connoisseur—except that you could touch and smell these still lifes.

> The last time my mother was upset with me was when she saw me talking with my children and opening my mail at the same time. She despised multitasking. She believed it was a way to miss life, to miss the gifts that come only when you give 100 percent of yourself to a task, a relationship, a moment.[15]

Arianna was her mother's daughter but was clearly not like her mother. Arianna is the queen of multitasking. Even the time she called me to tell me that she wanted me to write a book about her mother's life in the Greek resistance, I asked her if she were okay. There was a lot of heavy breathing amidst the invitation. As it turned out, Arianna was walking on her treadmill during the phone call.

This is typical of anyone who works with Arianna. She may be there with you in the room, but she's always doing several things at once. She may be giving an interview when the phone rings and one of her daughters calls. Arianna would never do one thing at a time. She doesn't have time for that, which is exactly what bothered her mother.

I attended the service for Elli Stassinopoulos, which was held in the backyard of the home where Elli lived with Arianna, sister Agapi, and her two granddaughters. It was a beautiful day and it was a day for Elli. When Arianna stood to talk about her mother, she broke down and cried. It was so touching to see a person who is labeled so often with impersonal titles such as media mogul, female entrepreneur, or digital diva show herself as anyone might—a daughter crying at the loss of her mother. It was the most vulnerable I've ever seen Arianna, something that is sadly missing from her media or brand image demeanor.

We all love strength in women and men, but we don't like cold or calculating types. Arianna's appears strong, but she can also appear defiant and heartless, as was illustrated when she was asked about a group of unpaid Huffington Post contributors from ArtScene and Visual Art Source. Bill Lasarow, publisher of both websites, said, "I am calling upon all others now contributing free content, particularly original content to the Huffington Post to also join us in this strike." Writers said they would stop contributing free content to her site and requested a nominal pay schedule. Her response was sharp: "The idea of going on strike when no one really notices. Go ahead, go on strike."

Arianna ran for governor of California in 2003 as a political independent. It was a culmination of a political climb to prominence that began in the mid-1990s. When she was married to Michael Huffington (1986-1997) she was a Republican wife, but not famous for her own policy pronouncements until she became close to Newt Gingrich, the GOP darling of the 1994 midterm elections who led the effort to frame a new "Contract with America." After she and Michael spent a then-record $28.3 million of his father's money unsuccessfully trying to unseat Democrat Dianne Feinstein in 1994, Newt Gingrich asked her to direct the Center for Effective Compassion as a Senior Fellow at his think tank, the Progress and Freedom Foundation.

*Time* magazine's Nina Burleigh profiled the meteoric rise of Arianna Huffington in "A Woman on the Verge," in which Arianna said, "I believe only Newt Gingrich can be the ideal standard-bearer for the Republican Party at this moment." [16] The *New York Times* called her a "Phoenix on the Right" because she had risen from the ashes of her husband's disastrous senatorial campaign. (In that campaign, Arianna and her connections to "John-Roger"[17] head of the Movement for Spiritual Inner Awareness, and the couple's undocumented nanny became of greater interest and entertainment than anything her husband said.) "Mrs. Huffington, one of the most ambitious, stylish and freely articulate spirits on the cantankerous Republican right, deftly handles her editor's questions on her latest syndicated column, then heads out into the silken hustle and rustle of Madison Avenue and back to her temporary writings digs at the Waldorf-Astoria. The flame-hair phoenix, a partner in one of the most celebrated political flops in her party's big 1994 victory, seems wondrously back on her perch."[18]

She supported the maverick Republican John McCain in 2000 but also encouraged close friend and liberal Democrat Warren Beatty to run in opposition to McCain's Democratic challengers Bill Bradley and Al Gore. In explaining her support for Beatty's run, she said, "We need a professional storyteller. We've become so atomized, and candidates are just addressing pocketbook issues. All the candidates are talking about prosperity, and nobody really does talk about the public good, about justice, and sacrifice, all those big things that we haven't heard since John F. Kennedy. And the need for someone to do that, for someone who can pull the nation around the fire and draw us together as we're being pulled apart, is all the more important with the presence of Buchanan, whom I consider very dangerous and don't underestimate at all."[19] She organized Shadow Convention 2000, whose motto was "A Citizens' Intervention in American Politics." Designed to shadow the Republican National Convention in Philadelphia and the Democratic National Convention in Los Angeles, the Shadow Convention was a partnership with progressive or bipartisan standard bearers such as Common Cause, Public Campaign, Global Exchange, and United for a Fair Economy. Arianna showed her ability to direct a herd of cats by deftly handling the competing egos and issues involved of so many organizations that normally do not garner such public attention or celebrity inclusion. That Shadow Convention "aired more ideas in an hour for fixing what ails America than the Republicans did in four days" wrote Russ Baker in *Columbia Journalism Review*.[20] It was a stunning success, and though it would be years before she took her ambitions online, the Shadow Convention social networks she built proved invaluable to setting up the architecture for the online salon and community building website that the Huffington Post became.

Her quest for the governor's job in California was her lowest point since she and Michael Huffington had been forced to explain how they lost $30 million dollars in his U.S. Senate run. Arianna entered the 2003 California race against another foreign-accented public figure, the action hero actor and former bodybuilder Arnold Schwarzenegger. She prided herself at being one of the first owners of a Toyota Prius Hybrid, while she taunted Arnold Schwarzenegger for driving his gas-guzzling Hummer. Unfortunately, the Shadow Convention had taught her the value of shadowing, but not of walking in a straight line around a microphone not intended for her. When she arrived by Prius on the day Arnold and wife Maria stepped out of his SUV to file recall campaign papers, she knocked over the microphone stand set up for Schwarzenegger to give remarks after leaving the county clerk's office. Her misstep led the newspapers the next day, as did the *Los Angeles Times* story that revealed she had paid less than $1,000 in taxes for 2001 and 2002.[21] (I want her tax accountant!) Those of us who knew her great success with the Shadow Convention thought that her best days were behind her and that she would retreat for good (into the shadows?) We underestimated her. The best days of the female Greek Icarus were yet to come; she would soon be silhouetted rising high against the new sun of the Internet.

In 2004 Arianna backed John Kerry for president and called him the natural one to follow Robert F. Kennedy's model, but soon expressed criticism of his passive posture in response to the Swift Boat Campaign; after his loss, she accused the Massachusetts senator's campaign of "choosing caution over boldness." By 2008 she excitedly endorsed the hope and change Democrat Barack Obama over the establishment Democrat Hillary Clinton.[22]

(Arianna has never been a fan of Bill, Hillary or any of the Clintonistas. One of her books, *Greetings from the Lincoln Bedroom*, is a political satire of all those overnight guests who clogged the Clinton White House at the height of its fundraising sleepovers.)

Arianna, as we can tell from her life's path and her biggest gamble with AOL, doesn't have playing it safe in her vocabulary—although I suppose, in reality, it is AOL that is gambling on her. She's already won her hand, and Tim Armstrong has handed her the pot.

Arianna's complicated political history, with its strong enthusiasms and unrealized ambitions, leads one to wonder what Arianna Huffington's true political intentions might be with AOL. As a media mogul, she's more a business conservative than a political liberal. But as the brand name face of The Huffington Post for the past six years, she's a royal member of the liberal left, whose *hoi polloi* (particularly its comments community) adored the Internet newspaper.

Some of her political enemies like to accuse her of being about as far left as one can travel on the political continuum. They use the "C" word to describe her, no, not the four-letter one, but the nine-letter word used on Charles Foster Kane. She's been called by a variety of Communist names from "Liberal Communist" to "Capitalist Communist." Arianna explains her political transformation this way:

> At Cambridge, I was passionate about debating. I was never to the far right. One of the debates I participated in was with John Kenneth Galbraith and William F. Buckley on the role of government and the markets. I was chosen to make the opening speech, arguing against an unregulated free market. On social issues, I was always pro-choice, pro-gay rights, pro-gun control.

My journey politically has always been about the role of government. My transformation had to do with my conclusion that in order to have a level playing field, we did need an activist government. That was the shift. It was a very specific transformation and happened after [Newt] Gingrich and the '94 Republican government.[23]

# CHICKS WITH CLICKS

AOL's CEO Tim Armstrong can hardly contain his excitement about working with the female entrepreneur Arianna Huffington. AOL has staked its livelihood on predominantly female consumers, "chicks with clicks," who are likely to respond favorably to the AOL brand and experience. An internal AOL memo Armstrong sent to all AOL staffers identifies influential women—and, specifically, Arianna—as keys to profit:

> The Huffington Post is core to our strategy and our 80:80:80 focus - 80% of domestic spending is done by women, 80% of commerce happens locally and 80% of considered purchases are driven by influencers. The influencer part of the strategy is important and will be potent.

> The Huffington Post is a strong influencer brand and it attracts a valuable audience, including a great focus on women's content. In addition, Arianna Huffington is a world-renowned expert on women's topics and issues, and has enabled The Huffington Post to grow rapidly by continually developing new audiences.[24]

AOL is staking its turnaround on Arianna's brand. She is renowned for many things: books, syndicated columns, marriage, political wife, spiritual guru, run for California governor, punditry, Shadow Conventions, Brentwood salons, celebrity friends and her namesake Internet website, all of which carry baggage and evoke both admiration and derision.

Was she successful with The Huffington Post? Yes, from a purely business perspective. Who in one's right mind outside of Arianna and her closest business associates would have calculated the value of HuffPost to be in the $300 million range? Somehow, in a matter of months, if one believes the narrative provided by Tim Armstrong and Arianna, a deal was made that would turn the digital media world upside down with envy and enmity.

Did was the sale of the HuffPot a success for Arianna, the personal brand? It depends on who you ask. Some of her far left critics call her a sell-out, while others say "Good for her," or "I'd do the same if I had the chance." Chris Hedges and Robert Scheer provide a great example of the range of reaction on the Left.

Scheer is the first person I ever met at the Arianna's home in 2000 after I decided to move to megacity Los Angeles from Henniker, New Hampshire, with its population of 3,000 and Thornton Wilder ambience. Scheer and his wife are longtime friends of Arianna and he has been one of Arianna's sparring partners on a popular politics program, "Left, Right & Center" produced by Santa Monica public radio network KCRW. Among LA progressives Scheer is a well-recognized leftist intellectual, with a long history of writing for the *Los Angeles Times*, and Scheer and I are "colleagues" in that we both teach as communication professors in the USC Annenberg School for Communication and Journalism. I also moderated a panel discussion on the Iraq war at the Los Angeles Times Festival of Books in 2007 that featured Scheer and Chris Hedges.

Scheer cheered on the business savvy of his friend and claimed there was "much ado about nothing" regarding the steady drumbeat of criticism around unpaid bloggers:

> Defenders of a free press should be thrilled that it is Huffington who is now merging with AOL rather than Matt Drudge, the unrivaled leader of Internet news whom I first met at Arianna's home when she was cozier with the right.

First off, and in defense of the use of unpaid bloggers, of which I happen to be one among the many who appear on a regular basis on the website The Huffington Post, we are not exploited. Blogging has opened up the traditional channels of reporting to include informed people with scholarly and experiential credibility who formerly were begging for the rare opportunity to appear on the carefully preserved Op-Ed plantation of leading newspapers. For most contributors, the Op-Ed page was never a serious source of income.[25]

Scheer's perspective was countered by Chris Hedges, the former Pulitzer-Prize winning writer for the *New York Times* and author of *War is a Force That Gives Us Meaning*. Hedges is a successful freelance writer who also writes a column for Scheer's online site, Truthdig.

Unlike Scheer, Hedges was nothing short of outraged by Arianna's actions with AOL:

Any business owner who uses largely unpaid labor, with a handful of underpaid, nonunion employees, to build a company that is sold for a few hundred million dollars, no matter how he or she is introduced to you on the television screen, is not a liberal or a progressive. Those who take advantage of workers, whatever their outward ideological veneer, to make profits of that magnitude are charter members of the exploitative class. Dust off your Karl Marx. They are the enemies of working men and women. And they are also, in this case, sucking the lifeblood out of a trade I care deeply about. It was bad enough that Huffington used her site for flagrant self-promotion, although the cult of the self has reached such dizzying proportions in American society that such behavior is almost expected. But there is an even sadder irony that this was carried out in the name of journalism.[26]

She is not someone who garners "ah shucks" shrug of the shoulders reactions, but rather "I love her" or "I hate her" pivot points. She may turn around AOL just fine, especially since she declares that moving to AOL is her last act, but many who admired

Huffington for creating a progressive online community during the Bush years loathed  business merger of 2011.

# PEDAGOGY OF THE OPPRESSED BLOGGER

In the spring of 2009 I was teaching at the S.I. Newhouse School of Public Communications in New York. Located on the campus of Syracuse University, the Newhouse School is considered among the top five best schools of communications in the United States, in the same company as Northwestern, Columbia, and the Annenberg Schools at USC and the University of Pennsylvania. Newhouse has an outstanding reputation in preparing students for careers in fields such as advertising, public relations, broadcast radio, television and film. The Newhouse School at Syracuse the reputation in the Northeast that the Annenberg School at USC has on the West Coast. I've met quite a few industry types in Hollywood and New York City who are graduates of either Newhouse or Annenberg.

While on vacation in Southern California that spring I received a phone call from a media and public affairs staff person at Newhouse. She asked me to provide some comments that would defuse a brouhaha that was brewing around the selection of Arianna Huffington as recipient of the 2009 Fred Dressler Lifetime Achievement Award. The Dressler Award is for a reporter, editor or publisher "who has made distinct, consistent, long-term and unique contributions to the public's understanding of the media."[27]

## The Russert Connection

Tim Russert, Washington bureau chief of NBC News and moderator of "Meet the Press" for seventeen years, had been announced as the 2008 Fred Dressler Lifetime Achievement Award recipient. Due to his sudden death on June 13, 2008, Russert was honored posthumously at the June 23rd awards. Anyone who knows insider media gossip wouldn't escape the irony of honoring Russert one year before Huffington. Tim Russert and his wife Maureen Orth were longtime objects of derision to Arianna and her ex-husband Michael Huffington. This bad blood between power couples began in November 1994 when *Vanity Fair* published a damning profile written by Orth about Arianna and her Senate-seeking husband, Michael Huffington. Orth implied that Michael, not Arianna, gave empty suits a bad reputation.[28] The husband was portrayed as a Chauncey Gardiner—the character portrayed by Peter Sellers in the 1979 film *Being There*—completely out of touch and disinterested in politics, while his wife Arianna served as Michael's ersatz brains and ambition. Orth, who had talked t people who had worked with either or both Huffingtons, claimed to be raising "the curtain on their own private Oz." She offered insights sixteen years ago that seem to echo Arianna's paradoxical brand image as the new editor in chief of AOL's Huffington Post Media Group:

> "There are two schools of thought about Arianna," says Mort Janklow, her U.S. agent on the Picasso book. "One is that it's all deliberate and calculated and she's ruthless. The other is that she really convinces herself beforehand. She sells herself first."

> There is definitely a spacey quality to both Huffingtons, which allows them to go after what they want unaffected by the impressions they leave behind. The pervasive sense is that everyone and everything is "of use": the Huffingtons schmooze you and then they use you.[29]

Orth asked Arianna for an explanation of the high turnover of staff in their $4.3 million Italianate mansion in Montecito outside

Santa Barbara, where the couple resided so that Michael could represent the more conservative wealthy voters of California's 22nd district. She got a self-revelation that did not emerge from other, more obsequious profiles:

> "I can be cruel," she finally admits. "Of course, I'm trying to improve myself every day and get better and be better—at whatever I'm doing." Arianna tells me she sees her life as similar to being on a train. "Being on a train and going home to God. And on the train is my family, the people I'm closest to. And outside the train, everything that happens to my life is scenery. Some of it is beautiful scenery. Some of it is ugly scenery ... but the train moves on."

Orth's *Vanity Fair* profile was a finalist for a National Magazine Award. Despite spending almost $30 million to unseat Diane Feinstein, Michael Huffington's political career was finished and his soon-to-be ex-wife would move on to new ambitions.

## Trouble Ahead

Newhouse Dean Lorraine Branham had explained the rationale for giving Huffington the 2009 Dressler Award in a press release: she "was ahead of the curve with HuffPo. She embraced the use of new media, but never forgot that no matter where or how you tell the story, content is still king. This is what we teach our students." These were seemingly innocuous comments, but as the date for the awards luncheon was fast approaching, some journalists were criticizing a professional communications school for awarding someone whose management exploited the labor of her thousands of unpaid bloggers.

One article in particular to which I was asked to reply was a damning piece by *Advertising Age* columnist Simon Dumenco that asked this question: "Why Is a Journalism School Honoring a Blog Mogul Who Thinks Journalists Should Work for Free?"

> And the award for the Most Bitterly Ironic Media Award goes to ... the Fred Dressler Lifetime Achievement Award, to be bestowed upon Arianna Huffington by Syracuse University's S.I. Newhouse School of Public Communications at the upcoming Mirror Awards luncheon in Manhattan.
>
> Congratulations, Arianna!
>
> Now please excuse me as I crawl under my desk and curl into the fetal position.
>
> Really, the school -- which exists to train journalists -- should know better than to honor a woman who thinks journalists should work for free![30]

Dumenco didn't just go after Huffington but also after Newhouse Dean Branham for daring to say that in Arianna's world "content is king."

> "Oh, give me a break! Content, in Arianna's world, is not king, and it never was. Link bait is king; opportunism is king."

The Newhouse School was none pleased with Dumenko for publishing his column one week before the Dressler Award was to be bestowed upon Arianna at the Harmonie Club in New York City. Given that I was an employee of the School that was bestowing the award, that I was a blogger for the publisher of the Huffington Post who was receiving the award, and that I had been personally invited by the dean of the same school to attend the event in Arianna's honor, I was reluctant to tell them that I thought Dumenco had a point.

# Arianna Is Crowned

FADE IN:

## HARMONIE CLUB – NEW YORK CITY – DAYTIME

A large room is crammed with tables for eight. A table of honor sits in the front middle of the room, the closest to the lectern. At this table sits the co-founder and editor-in-chief of The Huffington Post.

Lunch is over. Dessert is served. It is June 10, 2009.

She who is about to be honored is not a cover girl, girl next door, or his girl Friday. She is Arianna. Arianna, the Golden Girl of New Media. She is a woman of influence and affluence. Time has been kind to Arianna, for she not only runs her own media but also is talked about, reporter on, and profiled in the media at an astonishing rate. Her life--where she goes, whom she meets, where she speaks, what she tweets--is as important as any professional title. In fact, her life exceeds any resume detail. No one has lived a life like Arianna. Let's hear from Arianna and her admirers.[31]

BEGIN VIDEO

## The Huff

Arianna: "The Huffington Post is a combination of news aggregated from all sorts of sources, opinion (over 200 blogs and growing a day), and community."

Betsy Morgan, CEO, The Huffington Post: "It's a different type of site. We carry a lot of the same stories other news sites carry, but we carry those stories with a point of view, with a personality, with some style."

Rachel Maddow, The Rachel Maddow Show, MSNBC: "Huffington Post has become a defining brand in the world of news, politics, information, and how the Internet works and serves us, because it's a place where everybody stops in at least once a day, anytime you're engaged in any way with what's going on in the country."

Graydon Carter, Editor, *Vanity Fair*: "I think the online world has a great effect on politics, specifically this administration, their whole message. It's all gone out through the Internet."

Arianna: At first I invited all my friends, about five hundred people, everybody I considered interesting enough, whether they were well known or not, to start writing on The Huffington Post."

Tina Brown, Editor-in-Chief, The Daily Beast: "She has had such an interesting and diverse life that she's able to bring all her many contacts, her connections, and her instincts together in one place, to create a place that she can attract some interesting minds, new conversation, and a sense of political purpose."

Graydon Carter: "It's a sheer force of will on her part. I've never seen anybody do something so influential so quickly. And more power to her."

## Vox Populi

Arianna: "I've said that one of the problems with traditional journalism has been that it suffers from attention deficit disorder. Very important stories are broken on the front pages of newspapers and abandoned there. Online journalism suffers from obsessive-compulsive disorder. We pursue stories and pursue them, until there is an impact, until something happens. I love that."

Rachel Maddow: "When we talk about people trying to get their message out in politics now, people trying to make a statement, people trying to get their point of view across, it's almost taken for granted that they will use Huffington Post to do that."

Betsy Morgan: "In many ways Arianna and The Huffington Post are both reflecting and defining today's American culture and we're giving every reader a voice in that, and a chance to participate in that."

Tina Brown: "I think what's amazing about Arianna is that she's always been a pioneer. She does things out there, on the cutting edge. No one can stop her when she has a vision. She waited all her life to find a perfect medium for her and I think Huffington Post really expresses that."

Arianna: "I love my day job. I love what I'm doing at the moment. I don't really want to do anything different. I want to keep expanding The Huffington Post. And I feel very blessed to be working in journalism at this moment as so many of us are trying to reinvent it."

To this posted video, there were just four comments from the Huff community, but all positive, including the following:

Huffpost Community Moderator Chernynkaya: "I am hopelessly addicted to The Huffington Post! I check it SEVERAL times a day- God help me, I need a life. But if I had to choose an addiction, this one at least keeps me informed about all aspects of life. Also, the format is the best on the web. Thanks, guys. Great job!"

Marbur: "Being a rather mature female 76 plus years and now retired, I have The Huffington Post as my daily connection to the pulse of America and beyond. It offers such a feast for my curious appetite for what is going on in our ever changing world, I actually look forward to reading The Huffington Post every day. So many of your writers have become my favorites for content & style that I look forward to their columns.

Arianna, you are to be congratulated on the visionary concept of the Post and above all your success as you pushed forward to make it an informative & interesting place for journalism as it appears on my screen each day. Intelligence needs a voice & your intellect is giving us just that. Knowledge and truth is desperately needed in the world of journalism to counter the idiocy on our airways."

## Looking Back

What I didn't say in 2009 but what I would say in 2011 is that the Huffington Post model, that same model that made it so valued in early 2011 that it would be sold to AOL for $315 million, was a financial model that was built on a skeletal paid staff that benefited greatly from the unpaid labor of thousands upon thousands of bloggers. The biggest beneficiary was the brand known as Arianna Huffington. It would not and could not be any other way if one knows Arianna Huffington. She has a long history of spotting talent and using her personal charm to get people to sign on to her endeavors with no money down (at least not hers). As the value of the endeavor skyrockets, all the investment in blood, sweat and tears comes back to the founder.

Much of the Huffington Post "content is king" content consists of aggregated repost-it notes from paid sources as well as original posts by bloggers who write for free. For our free labor (whistling while we work), bloggers get visibility and distribution of our writings. One HuffPo blogger, Mayhill Fowler, gained a great deal of fame during the 2008 campaign when she published a news-breaking piece that included remarks by presidential candidate Barack Obama referencing voters in the upcoming Pennsylvania primary. Fowler was in attendance at an April 6, 2008 San Francisco fundraiser. Obama said, "You go into some of these small towns in Pennsylvania, and like a lot of small towns in the Midwest, the jobs have been gone now for 25 years and nothing's replaced them. And they fell through the Clinton Administration, and the Bush Administration, and each successive administration has said that somehow these communities are going to regenerate and they have not. And it's not surprising then they get bitter, they cling to guns or religion or antipathy to people who aren't like them or anti-immigrant sentiment or anti-trade sentiment as a way to explain their frustrations."

Mayhill wrote that, "Obama made a problematic judgment call in trying to explain working class culture to a much wealthier audience. He described blue collar Pennsylvanians with a series of what in the eyes of Californians might be considered pure negatives: guns, clinging to religion, antipathy, xenophobia. I'm not sure this is what at least this lot of Californians needed to hear about Pennsylvanians. Such phrases can reinforce negative stereotypes among Californians, who are a people in a state already surfeited with a smug sense of superiority and, as an ironic consequence, a parochialism and insularity at odds with the innovation, prosperity and openness for which California is rightly known."[32]

For her posting of Obama's remarks and her subsequent comments, Fowler was accused of being a Hillary Clinton plant at the fundraiser or even a spy for the Republicans. Ultimately her HuffPo blog, "No Surprise That Hard-Pressed Pennsylvanians Turn Bitter," received over 6,000 comments and elevated the citizen-journalist status of bloggers, or at least caught the attention of presidential candidates who may have thought that they were safely away from the media's scrutiny at a private fundraiser.

For bringing so much attention to The Huffington Post bloggerverse, Fowler made an ill-fated request to Arianna Huffington that she start receiving some payment for her work. The request was turned down and Fowler went public with her resignation, writing, "at the end of the day, that is the crux: I want to be paid for my time and effort—or at a minimum, to get a little remuneration in return for the money I spend myself in order to do original reportage. I would not expect to be paid for punditry. The Huffington Post business model is to provide a platform for 6,000 opinionators to hold forth. Point of view is cheap."[33] A Huffington Post spokesman sniffed, "How do you resign from a job you never had?"[34]

The "oppressed blogger" meme would never disappear.

# AOL: "AFFLUENCE ONLINE"?

To prosper, a theater in London needed to draw as many as two thousand spectators a day—about 1 percent of the city's population—two hundred or so times a year, and to do so repeatedly against stiff competition. To keep customers coming back, it was necessary to change the plays continually. Most companies performed at least five different plays in a week, sometimes six, and used such spare time as they could muster to learn and rehearse new ones.[35]

> Charles Foster Kane: Look, Mr. Carter. Here is a three-column headline in the Chronicle. Why hasn't the Inquirer a three-column headline?
>
> Carter: News wasn't big enough.
>
> Charles Foster Kane: Mr. Carter, if the headline is big enough, it makes the news big enough.

On February 1, 2011, just days before the post-Super Bowl AOL announcement, Business Insider published a 58-page document called "The AOL Way."[36] It revealed AOL's performance-enhancing master plan to create more stories that aggregate well. More in this case should not be confused with better. The document included goals such as these:

> Increase stories per month from 33,000 to 55,000 by April 2011.
>
> Video stories should go from 4% to 70%.
>
> Nearly all stories (95%) should be "SEO friendly." [search-engine optimized]

Editors were exhorted to exploit trending topics, such as this gem:

> Use editorial insight to determine production. Ex: "Macaulay Culkin" & "Mila Kunis" are trending because they broke up → write story about Macaulay Culkin and Mila Kunis.[37]

What "The AOL Way" reveals is just reinforced by marketing communciations from AOL Advertising, which anyone can look up online. Here is where the raison d'être of the company comes to light.

**It Is Elitist.** AOL does not cater to the *vox populi*, but to the *vox electissimus:* "The money trail leads here. AOL Advertising reaches the most affluents online: 88%."[38] As AOL says, "We know how the other half lives," ostensibly the better half since the affluents label refers to American households that make over $100,000, the Top 15% of households. *Vox populi, vox Dei* (the voice of the people is the voice of God) may be a damned maxim in this marketplace of ideas. AOL boasts "a trust compact," but only with affluents: "So when they're online, more affluents trust AOL to help them make living the good life what it's supposed to be—good."

Look around you, America. Do you see that good life eroding? Well, it's not eroding in AOL's advertising suites.

**It is Potentially Schizophrenic.** A problem for AOL-HuffPo is how it will avoid becoming a schizophrenic brand where communication messages contradict each other. It may have already. AOL's CEO Tim Armstrong is essentially a marketing and sales guy from Google. He is not the quasi-academic social scientist Arianna who has zigged and zagged through capitalist America on a messianic mission. Arianna is noted for books with titles like

*Right Is Wrong: How The Lunatic Fringe Hijacked America, Shredded The Constitution and Made Us All Less Safe, Pigs at the Trough* and *Third World America*, which I applaud since I'm responsible for *The Arrogance of American Power* and *Propaganda, Inc.* But I'm not heading the Huffington Post Media Group at AOL. Accompanying chapter headings like "Nightmare on Main Street" and "America the ~~Beautiful~~ Dilapidated",comes this from her 2010 book, *Third World America*:

> "Washington rushed to the rescue of Wall Street but forgot about Main Street … One in five Americans unemployed or underemployed. One in nine families unable to make the minimum payment on their credit cards. One in eight mortgages in default or foreclosure. One in eight Americans on food stamps. Upward mobility has always been at the center of the American Dream … that promise has been broken … The American Dream is becoming a nightmare."[39]

Armstrong and Huffington are quite the nightclub act, but they do seem to contradict each other in their messaging. At one event, Arianna talked in spiritual tomes like "humanizing everything" at AOL and creating nap rooms for AOL staff. Armstrong quipped, "Yes, where you can nap from 10 p.m. until 6 in the morning." Is it going to be "Arianna's Way" or "The AOL Way" or a combination of both? In the spirit of Clairol's hairdresser, only the shareholders know for sure.

**It Is More Feminine Than Masculine.** AOL boasts that it knows what women want since women spend more time on AOL sites than almost anywhere else on the Web (23.9 minutes per day to be precise.) AOL Advertising is said to reach over 90% of women using the Web. While men are also on AOL, they are not the primary target for the AOL-Huffington Post merger. Arianna's savvy about knowing what women want, and, according to Tim

Armstrong, "being an expert on women's issues," makes it even more likely that AOL will continue to market predominantly to women, who make the most purchases online or based on information they read online. As James Rainey said about AOL, "they have a sense that the woman with the honeyed Greek accent provides them one of the quickest portals to gossip, sports, fashion, books, religion and more."[40]

**It is All About The Money**. As AOL says, "Money talks. It also uses the Internet." AOL makes no bones about its target audience: "AOL does well with the well to do."

**It's All About the Brands.** Tim Armstrong says that the merger with Huffington Post will be brand-driven. "People are writing a lot about content factories and those things. This [merger] is about brands.... We are working on brands that are going to stand the test of time in the next version of the Internet."

In yet another leaked memo, Armstrong talked about AOL's direction after acquiring The Huffington Post. It's not very journalism-friendly; the word journalism is mentioned once, while the full memo cites the word brand 35 times.[41]

> Roughly 60 days after agreeing to terms on The Huffington Post deal, we are ready to play offense on the future of our content business with the full integration of The Huffington Post and our AOL Media properties. Brands are how consumers navigate the world and we are continuing to build our portfolio of significant brands for the digital age. AOL is a global and trusted brand and today we are announcing some changes to our brand portfolio that will allow us to significantly scale our reach and our impact.
>
> Our consumers are already seeing meaningful examples of the value in the integration of AOL and The Huffington Post - we've cross-pollinated content across our properties, incorpo-

rated HuffPost's social sharing tools on AOL, added Devil ads to HuffPost, and added AOL brands to the HuffPost nav bar. Most importantly, we have started to work together as one passionate team, committed to building best-in-class brands for our users.

In the words of the immortal Moody Blues,

My world is spinning around,

Everything is lost that I found.

People run, come ride with me,

Let's find another place that's free.

Ride, ride my see-saw,

# ARIANNA'S ROSEBUD

> Give me the child until he is seven and I will give you
> the man.

> *--Jesuit saying*

I don't have the privilege of knowing much of anything about Arianna Huffington's childhood. Anything I've ever read about her background seems to start from her education in England at the University of Cambridge. To observe her from where she sits now makes it even harder to imagine her formative years. Did she have the incredible drive and stamina as a young girl that she shows now? Did she engender as much tough criticism as a child or young adult as we see now? I would love to have known Citizen Arianna at seven or even double seven. "Give me Arianna until she is seven and I will give you the woman." What did she learn from her father and her mother together before they separated? What impact did her father leaving the family home have on the father-daughter relationship? What lessons did Elli teach Arianna and her sister Agapi about making it in a man's world or even another country? How does her mother's influence, her closest female connection, still connect to how Arianna operates today?

The Arianna Huffington of the post-Huffington Post merger with AOL is like a typecast heroine from the golden days of celluloid—brazen, bold, flippant, funny, smart, she's a woman who doesn't suffer fools gladly. Cross her and she'll mark you off her Blackberry contacts or Twitter feed like dead air. Make her shine and she'll be loyal, but don't try to outshine her—ever. If you do, see above. If Hollywood ever gives us "Citizen Arianna," I can guarantee you that Sandra Bullock won't be considered for the part.

So, who really is Arianna Stassinopoulos Huffington, and how much do we really care? I care because she is directing the flight patterns of one of the biggest supersonic jets in the stratosphere of digital online media.

In her memo, "When HuffPo Met AOL: A Merger of Visions," she described the purchase of The Huffington Post by AOL as boarding a whole new mode of transportation:

> Far from changing our editorial approach, our culture, or our mission, this moment will be for HuffPost like stepping off a fast-moving train and onto a supersonic jet. We're still traveling toward the same destination, with the same people at the wheel, and with the same goals, but we're now going to get there much, much faster.[42]

The transportation metaphors in which Arianna views her life just keeping getting faster, perhaps to reflect the blur of the digital age.

This may be AOL-HuffPost's Sputnik moment, but it could be the public's Edsel or New Coke if we don't understand the deep impact that this merger will have on the Internet user. If successful, Arianna's digital prints will be all over the look, feel and content of our online world from movie reviews, to celebrity gossip updates, to tech world innovations, to local stories via Patch, to international media. From the looks of the Twitpics and tweetings on @ariannahuff, this is not a woman who appears to be slowing down to contemplate the social and cultural implications of her new media endeavors. I see a lot of pictures that say "Where in the world is Arianna?" and "Who is Arianna in a picture with today?" but alas, no Rosebud moments. Alas, we don't even know what her "rosebud" word will be.

The unpaid bloggers and their supporters who are boycotting the post-AOL merger Huffington Post remind me of that famous Russian toast: "And here is to our futile endeavor." As much as I hate the sneering tone of "go ahead and strike, no one will notice," Arianna Huffington is just cashing in on her mind-boggling ability to get thousands of sun-seekers like myself to write for free in exchange for being a featured link in her media kingdom.

Sharing that I blog for the Huffington Post has had its unpaid perquisites over the years. I'm aligned with the academic world and higher education in communications and political science, so telling people within these circles that I am a blogger for the Huffington Post evokes an impressive reaction, at least from those left liberal progressives who dominate the social sciences of the academy. (I won't comment on how my right-leaning friends have responded.)

In the academy we are so used to a lot of unpaid accolades (pen sets, certificates, attagirls and attaboys) that it seems laughable to think that one could expect any payment from an aggregated hyperlink. After all, if you agree to write for free, as I did, you cannot turn around and demand to be paid later.

There is no question that Arianna Huffington benefitted enormously from the myriad of perspectives at her site and this helped to boost her company's value ten-fold before its sale to AOL. If one is truly miffed about not receiving some stipend like $1,000 to name just an arbitrary number, then by all means stop writing for her exploitative website. To assume that writing for Huffington post wouldn't benefit Arianna Huffington financially is not to know Arianna Huffington. She's not going to venture into any endeavor that doesn't monetarily benefit her. Further, she is accurate in saying that no one will notice a boycott. She knows that 9,000 disparate bloggers will not unify over this issue; furthermore, another 9,000 or 99,000 bloggers wait in the wings to replace the dearly departed.

The AOL-HuffPo merger has led to one academic institution, UC-Santa Barbara, surveying Huffington Post bloggers about their response to the merger. Researchers at the Carsey-Wolf Center Media Industries Project (MIP) asked a fraction of the 9,000 bloggers to answer the following questions:

> Do you feel you should receive part of the $315 million AOL used to purchase the Huffington Post?
>
> Do you feel that the Huffington Post's brand has changed since the merger with AOL?
>
> How would you compare the conditions at the Huffington Post to other sites you have blogged for?
>
> Some have raised concerns about the labor arrangement bloggers have with The Huffington Post. In your opinion, what do you think is the best way for bloggers to address the issue of compensation for digital labor?

Unsurprisingly, mixed feelings toward the HuffPost/AOL merger emerged from the MIP survey, but what didn't emerge was a collective walkout. Nearly all bloggers (96%) perceived unpaid blogger writings as equally valuable, if not more valuable, than the work of paid editors at Huffington Post. Nearly seven out of ten bloggers (69%) felt that they should have shared in the $315 million purchase by AOL of HuffPo. Just over half of the bloggers (54%) supported some type of pay scale for bloggers as well as some collective action to assert their value. Despite feelings of personal value contrasted with unpaid lower status, nearly all (92%) surveyed said that they would continue to write for The Huffington Post because it serves as a platform for personal promotion of their work. Nevertheless, the UCSB writing team recommended some type of merit-based pay scale: "Accordingly, employers such as HuffPo might wish to design compensation models that include a range of monetary and promotional payments. Furthermore, it seems important for such employers to develop technologies that can discriminate between regular contributors who can build and generate a following and therefore add substantial value to their sites, and those that only post occasionally."[43]

The survey notes that the stereotype of the unpaid blogger of past sitting in front of his computer writing "just for fun" doesn't make as much sense now that a blogging-centered site like The Huffington Post illustrates that significant profit can emerge from the collective value of its bloggers' contributions. Bloggers themselves remain conflicted about their content value. If it is worth payment, then why continue to write for free?

As a current writer for The Huffington Post, I can offer a personal explanation for this dichotomy. Though I have my own personal namesake website, Twitter page, and Facebook wall, nothing compares to the distribution reach of The Huffington Post. If I post something on my website, I do not have enough web traffic to my site to replicate distribution. If I post to my HuffPo page, I'm assured that many other sites will republish my article. My reach is much greater through the search engine optimization of a powerhouse like the AOL-sponsored Huffington Post.

Like many longtime bloggers at The Huffington Post, I wasn't happy with the sale to AOL It was a sell-out by Arianna Huffington, who knows all too well that for every blogger writing for her now, there are probably ten others ready and willing to replace that blogger. This is why she continues to scoff at the idea that bloggers for Huffington have any greater value than any other blogger. As she puts it, we're just hucksters hawking our work like any person who might appear on television to promote an idea or product. It is true that whenever I've appeared on television to talk about a book or give a talk I haven't expected any paid compensation. After all, I'm not at the level of a celebrity endorser or paid media analyst, many of whom make a good living from their regular appearances. But there are perks that have come with my major media appearances, including transportation and travel compensation. So should I refuse any future appearances because my perceived value doesn't match a media booker's value of me? No, I happily agree to do these appearances because I know that they help whenever I'm asked to speak at certain venues. It leads to introductions like the following: "Dr. Snow has appeared on major media like CNN, MSNBC, Fox News Channel, C-SPAN, and National Public Radio." Audiences tend to up the value of a speaker who has the TV glow about her.

Mixed feelings toward Brand Arianna and the AOL-HuffPo marriage will remain. But should we nsome of the ongoing criticism of Arianna Huffington is driven by gender bias. We still aren't comfortable with women who dominate in business and politics, and Arianna has done both. She is not full of traditional feminine humility about occupying so much of the publicity spotlight. Why should *that* matter, you ask? Because women from Athens to Atlanta are still conditioned to be less assertive and outspoken about their goals and ambitions. There are exceptions to this acculturation, but undoubtedly Arianna's strong elbow approach to doing business rubs many the wrong way because that's just not the way feminine women are supposed to act. We women are well conditioned to defer to those in charge or, if we are really in charge, to do it in the background without claiming credit. Arianna is front-and-center about everything she does. She craves the spotlight and, as we know, sometimes knocks down press microphones in the process.

When I think about my all too short friendship with Arianna's mom Elli, I think of a woman who was as strong, if not stronger, than her daughter Arianna, but who ruled in the background. The Elli I knew had no desire to be famous or to control the fore-ground. She quietly captured one's attention at a pace much slower and without much fanfare. She was the kind one would sit with and perhaps massage her foot or hand. She had time for you. This is the image of a more traditional woman, who, had she been born later in the 20th century may very well have become a leading pubic figure in her own right. Instead, she put all her energies into the success of her two daughters and was witness to at least one be-coming quite famous..

Arianna Huffington's new perch atop AOL's flagship division places her among the leading media figures of the 21st Century. The digital diva has succeeded financially beyond anyone's expectations. Throughout her public life, she's been able to rise above setbacks and above steady criticism from onlookers who view her as a soul-less self-promoter.

A fundamental problem remains for her as the two companies become one. Public opinion has been strongly divided about the woman behind the merger. Tim Armstrong at AOL appears to be getting smaller in stature and import as Arianna's height and power seem to be getting stronger. He cannot hold his own as well as she in any interview they've given about the merger. History suggests that CEOs whose subordinates outshine them either rectify the situation or move on. Yet Arm isn't taking as much of the heat for the merger as Arianna for two reasons: (1) so many people already dislike the company; and (2) AOL has been seen for some time as a company associated with the last century, when dialup was king and every person in America received those damnable software CDs.

Arianna is taking the most heat. She is, after all, the face of the new content at AOL. But her reputation is a two-edged sword. To some, she wears a tyrant's crown; to others, a tiara. She's also never managed so many properties or people in her life. Former Huffington Post or household employees with juicy tidbits on her charming facade-shattering management style will continue to surface. I've been around Arianna enough to know that she is immune to any attacks, which makes her more like a cartoon superhero zapping any jabs or darts that come her way. It is impressive. But will her bad press leak into the public "all is good" feel at AOL?

It's already happening. The honeymoon is over for Huffington and Armstrong, if online tongues wagging are true. Take, for instance, a recent publication, "AOL INSIDER: Here Are 12 Reasons Why The AOL-Huffington Post Merger Is Going Down In Flames (AOL)." Among the twelve were several I've observed: an editorial staff at HuffPo that is extremely inexperienced with steering a huge dinosaur like AOL and Arianna's strong personality and "the same rules don't apply to me" approach rubbing staff the wrong way. A particularly foreboding statement emerged that titled toward hellion over heroine: "The editorial team is miserable and views Arianna as unpredictable and her leadership unsteady. Several editors are racing to close book deals to write the *Devil Wears Prada* of the digital age. Others are aggressively pitching unflattering profiles to New York Magazine, Vanity Fair, and the LA

Times. The lack of maturity and loyalty among editors is stunning – even those close to her are extremely negative behind her back – which is surprising because she has done a great job taking care of her people."[44]

There was once a supersized ego on the West and East Coast whose wealth and presence were the toast of Hollywood. No one could touch him. His San Simeon castle occupied space one-half the size of Rhode Island. One-name A-List actors attended his parties: Chaplin, Fairbanks, Gable, Pickford, Shearer, along with studio moguls like L.B. Mayer and Jack Warner. He controlled the media and partied with the cultural elite. In his heyday, one of every five Americans read one of his newspapers. San Simeon was his real kingdom but newspapers were his virtual kingdom. Reputations were made or killed under his tutelage.

Douglas Fairbanks asked him why he didn't go into the movies. His reply: "I thought of it, but I decided against it, because I realize that you can crush a man with journalism, and you can't with motion pictures."[45] William Randolph Hearst knew that the power of the printed word was more powerful than the sword. But more than that, a recycled story with a Hearst byline was even better: make it *his* story with so much more sensational style, boldness, and turn-the-page appeal that a reader would forget that it didn't originate in a Hearst paper. Hearst would take all the credit.

His staff called itself "the wrecking crew." They worked around the clock, smoking cigars in dark lighting, churning out story after story, many true, but others trumped up with embellished details. A Hearst newspaper had something for everyone: a moralistic editorial by Hearst and a harlot scandal on page one. Fatty Arbuckle didn't stand a chance when the Hearst *Examiner* went after his rape and murder charge with a circulation vengeance. The obese comedic actor who earned a million dollars in 1921 was portrayed as a lecherous monster preying on the diminutive bit player Virginia Rappe. All we remember today are the headline-screaming charges that ran on the front pages of Hearst newspapers for months, not the acquittal and public apology to Arbuckle. Sales were so brisk that Hearst was said to boast it "sold more newspapers than the sinking of the Lusitania."[46] It wouldn't be the last time that a newspaper chain became a serial killer.

When Hearst newspapers came to dominate the American West, he headed for New York to take on Joseph Pultzer's world and *World*. His *New York Journal American* would overtake Pulitzer in circulation by the highest form of flattery: imitation. One biographer, Mrs. Fremont Older, wife of Hearst's former San Francisco editor, said, "[Hearst] had made up his mind to have a paper as much as possible like the *World*, only he would out-*World* the *World* and out-Pulitzer Pulitzer...."[47]

Hearst wasn't satisfied. He tried and failed to become New City mayor, then New York's governor, then Democratic presidential nominee in pursuit of the top prize in America: the White House. His ambition was unstoppable, but his goals were elusive. The press on Hearst was a very mixed bag, as was revealed by *Time* magazine in a review of several Hearst biographies released in succession in 1936, five years before the showing of the fictionalized biopic *Citizen Kane*.

Today Hearst is the keystone of American fascism, the integrating point …. around which political reaction is attempting to develop.

> —*Imperial Hearst: A Social Biography,* by
> Ferdinand Lundberg, charter member of the
> American Newspaper Guild

All his life he has worked on behalf of death—the death of personal integrity, the death of decent journalism, the death of honest patriotism—and now ultimately death will take its own.

> —*Hearst: Lord of San Simeon,* by Oliver Carlson &
> Ernest Sutherland Bates Carlson & Bates, based on
> a series of articles for the Leftist magazine
> *Common Sense*

He still sees through the eyes of youth. . . . Time has not dulled his sense of news. He wants to make people laugh, cry, to stir them with his own eagerness for news and his passion for the greatness of America.

> —*William Randolph Hearst: American, by* Mrs. Fremont
> Older, wife of *Examiner* editor Fremont Older

Arianna Huffington leads a fabulous life, just like William Randolph Hearst. She tweets her travels from Los Angeles to New York, San Francisco to London. Her over 600,000 Twitter followers (as of June 2011) monitor her supersonic jet lifestyle with envy and awe. She is the most internationally recognized Greek woman since Maria Callas sang opera and Jackie became an Onassis. There is as yet no book-length tome on the life of Arianna, but one is sure to follow soon. And when the backlash coalesces, it will include a puzzling portrait of Citizen Arianna that has risen since she sold The Huffington Post to AOL in February 2011.

"The Newspaper Guild is calling on unpaid writers of the Huffington Post to withhold their work in support of a strike launched by Visual Art Source in response to the company's practice of using unpaid labor. In addition, we are asking that our members and all supporters of fair and equitable compensation for journalists join us in shining a light on the unprofessional and unethical practices of this company."[48]

"The queen of aggregation is, of course, Arianna Huffington, who has discovered that if you take celebrity gossip, adorable kitten videos, posts from unpaid bloggers and news reports from other publications, array them on your Web site and add a left-wing soundtrack, millions of people will come. How great is Huffington's instinctive genius for aggregation? I once sat beside her on a panel in Los Angeles (on — what else? — The Future of Journalism). I had come prepared with a couple of memorized riffs on media topics, which I duly presented. Afterward we sat down for a joint interview with a local reporter. A moment later I heard one of my riffs issuing verbatim from the mouth of Ms. Huffington. I felt so . . . aggregated."[49]

"The Huffington Post is a brilliantly packaged product... to grasp its business model, though, you need to picture a galley rowed by slaves and commanded by pirates."[50]

I can't wait to see the movie.

# FAIL-SAFE?

"If you buy AOL stock right now you're going to make a lot of money."

*—AOL stock-holding executive, Arianna Huffington*

Arianna Huffington is a repeat failure. *Success* magazine says it's so. The irony isn't difficult to grasp, when one thinks that this current CEO of the Huffington Post Media Group appears to be calling the shots for the big shots on the World-Wide Web and nabbing some of the best writers of the *New York Times* to come work for her at AOL. But back in ancient times, circa September 2010, *Success*'s Mary Vinnedge interviewed the über-available interviewee about the many life failures that spurred on her ambitions.

"Failure is an option for Arianna Huffington," wrote Vinnedge. She failed at running for California governor in 2003. She failed thirty-six times at getting a follow-up book published to her first successful book, *The Female Woman*, which she published in 1973 at the unripe age of 23. Never an insider in the UK or US with her thick Greek accent, she persevered because failure was not a permanent option. It was something to overcome. Once again, Arianna's mother Elli appears to have been the most influential in helping Arianna overcome life's setbacks.

> My mother instilled in me that failure was not something to be afraid of, that it was not the opposite of success. It was a steppingstone to success. So I had no fear of failure.
>
> Perseverance is everything. I don't give up. Everybody has failures, but successful people keep on going...She was my life mentor.[51]

Her father, Konstantinos Stassinopoulos, divorced Elli in 1961 when Arianna was just 11. Six years later, the 17-year-old was studying economics at Cambridge, after much personal sacrifice on the part of her mother, who knew what a degree from a world-renowned university would do for her daughter's abilities and ambitions. It was while at Cambridge that Arianna honed her legendary elocution skills and rose to the heights of prestige when she became president of the Cambridge Union debate team. London was also where she got her start as a public media figure. She was still only in her twenties when she appeared on television going head-to-head in debates with men, notably William F. Buckley, with whom she had an embarrassing televised appearance, and Bernard Levin, who would become her intellectual mentor and companion. These early TV appearances were highly unusual for a young woman. She showed that she could hold her own with middle-aged men who were much more accustomed to debates with each other than with an attractive redheaded female with a Greek accent.

Arianna's stunning beauty and poise made her stand out from the crowd, and people wanted to be in her company, even though she didn't have money power in her twenties. Her power emerged from the combustible combination of youth, intelligence, sociability, and beauty. At Cambridge, she was well on her way to becoming the woman of global influence that she is most definitely today at 60. As a worldly socialite in London, hosting regular salons with her popular Greek mother and sister Agapi, Arianna learned about "the social network" offline decades before she conquered the social network online.

Given the strong foundation in believing in oneself that Arianna had from the time she was a young woman, is there anything that could cause her to fail now? It is hard to imagine anything but continued success now that she is at the level of "filthy rich" with her sale of The Huffington Post to AOL. She is perched at the heights of media chiefdom. There is really nowhere else to go in her achievements other than overseeing the global takeover of planet online by AOL. But little cracks are emerging that may yet test her unflappable reputation.

One faultline is her supreme confidence, which borders on arrogance. She laughs off any criticism, whether from Bill Keller, executive editor at the *New York Times*, or from any bloggers who argue that her success came from walking on their backs. Keller, who was just replaced by media veteran Jill Abramson, had a personal disdain for Arianna that seemed disproportionate to reality. Some at *The New York Times*—that is, those who still work there and who weren't snatched up by HuffPo—have had to tip their old media hats to the new media titan. Love her or hate her, you don't fail to honor the enormous influence of the Great Greek Media Aggregator.

Unlike Keller, Abramson has demonstrated a much softer approach to Arianna as the new giant of media aggregators—a truce, at least for now. This is due in part to the fact that Abramson is her own media titan. She has made media history as the first female executive editor at *The New York Times*, something that took the esteemed media institution 160 years to achieve. This accomplishment puts Abramson in the same media stratosphere of Huffington. In an interview with CNN on June 2, 2011, Abramson, who was quickly dubbed "The Gray Lady's new leading lady," spelled out that the era of bad blood between HuffPo and the NYT was over: "I've known Arianna Huffington since the early '90s in Washington—she is an inventive person. I certainly don't want to be in a war with her."[52]

During an interview with TechCrunch founder Michael Arrington in New York, Arianna touted AOL stock. "If you buy AOL stock right now you're going to make a lot of money."[53] This is by one measure a confident gesture and it did bump up AOL's one-day value by 2%, but it was also is a potential violation of SEC rules that prohibit manipulation of the markets by stock-holding employees. Despite these early warning signs, Tim Armstrong said there is no looking back for AOL from its marriage to Arianna: "The intersection of information and commerce is a very powerful place to be."[54]

Arianna Huffington has left the free-wheeling environment of the blogger extraordinaire where she had the liberty to say whatever she wanted with little, if any, risk of violating securities laws. She answered to no one but her Huffington Post board, and, according to media reports, not very well, either. Now she must take into account her fellow shareholders as a major investor in a private company traded on Wall Street. This is new territory for a woman who just a few years earlier managed to explain away two years of paying fewer than $1,000 in taxes while on her quick-stop run for governor of California.

# SLEEPING HER WAY TO THE TOP

Arianna Huffington has been accused of many things, including doing anything she could to reach the pinnacle of power. For powerful women this has often meant sleeping their way to the top of fame and fortune with attachments to powerful men. If this holds for Arianna, then she is certainly not the first woman to do so and there is no law she has violated by doing so. One could even argue that she didn't need to attach herself early on to powerful men because she was a powerful woman in her own right. As a media aggregator who understands the value of the controversial headline, Arianna recently went on MSNBC and was asked by ad-man Donny Deutsch if women should employ any "old school stereotypes" to get where they wanted. Her response, one of her legendary zingers, was to say that women "should sleep their way to the top." Then she explained what she really meant:

> I mean literally sleep. I think women need to redefine success. We need to stop feeling that success is driving ourselves into the ground, working around the clock, never having time for yourself, never having any balance in your life and having a heart attack in your 50s.

> I think it's going to be a major, major role that women have to play. And literally sleeping, recharging – we talk about it all the time, taking time for ourselves, making sure we do what we need to do for our families. I think we're going to be more effective, more creative, more productive. It's the exact opposite of the main way we've done things and look where it's gotten us.[55]

Despite her seemingly boundless energy on display at age 60, she is a strong advocate for women sleeping their way to the top of success. Anyone who follows her on Twitter knows that she is a tweet meme fanatic about #sleep. But when Arianna first announced the HuffPost-AOL merger, she described the event in a breathless analogy, "like stepping off a fast-moving train and onto a supersonic jet." Despite her latest maternal directive toward women getting more sleep, it's doubtful she's getting much of her own with all the musical chairs of incoming and outgoing staff, new divisions, and global expansion.

I'm losing sleep, too. I'm picturing every last breathing journalist being wooed by Citizen Arianna with a lofty promise of quality journalism and endless aggregation. It's a supersonic jet for them, but maybe a slow walk to independent media oblivion for the rest of us. Rosebud.

# ENDNOTES

1 D.B. Grady, "*Citizen Kane* at 70: The Legacy of the Film and Its Director," *The Atlantic*, May 3, 2011;
http://www.theatlantic.com/entertainment/archive/2011/05/citizen-kane-at-70-the-legacy-of-the-film-and-its-director/237029/
2 Jeff Bercovici, "NY Times Editor Bill Keller: The Exit Interview," Forbes.com, June 2, 2011. http://blogs.forbes.com/jeffbercovici/2011/06/02/ny-times-editor-bill-keller-the-exit-interview/
3 Bill Keller, "All the Aggregation That's Fit to Aggregate," *New York Times*, March 13, 2011. http://www.nytimes.com/2011/03/13/magazine/mag-13lede-t.htm?_r=4
4 "The Night Before Christmas" by Clement Clarke Moore.
5 Note, however, that despite the tall claims of the Texans about maximum capacity, the University of Michigan stadium drew an average of 111,825 actual visitors for seven football Saturdays in 2010, the last year of the tragic Rodriguez era, http://bentley.umich.edu/athdept/stadium/stadtext/mattend.htm
6 Oliver Burkeman, "Blogwars: Clooney clashes with Huffington over 'approved' posting," *The Guardian*, March 17, 2006.
7 "AOL CEO Tim Armstrong's 2010 Compensation Drops 40% to $15.3 Million, Hollywood Reporter, April 7, 2011.
http://www.hollywoodreporter.com/news/aol-ceo-tim-armstrong-s-176077
8 Sharon Waxman, "Exclusive: Arianna Huffington Will Not Make AOL a Leftie Blog," The Wrap, February 7, 2011. http://www.thewrap.com/media/column-post/exclusive-huffington-will-not-make-aol-leftie-blog-video-24565
9 A woman of two political minds. The Guardian, Thursday 7 August 2003. http://www.guardian.co.uk/world/2003/aug/07/usa.marktran
10 Emily Ngo, "Arianna Huffington: The making of a mogul,"*am New York*; http://www.amny.com/urbanite-1.812039/arianna-huffington-the-making-of-a-mogul-1.2683922.
11 http://ariannaonline.huffingtonpost.com/columns/column.php?id=400
12 Arianna Huffington, "New Hampshire 2000: The Battle for the Independents." http://ariannaonline.huffingtonpost.com/columns/column.php?id=227
13 Philip Messing, "Huffington risked lives: foe," *New York Post*, January 12, 2011.
14 Aaron Bowden, "Primary Callers." *Concord Monitor*, July 5, 1999, A1.
15 "International Women's Day: Life (and Work) Lessons Every Woman Should Learn, Arianna Huffington, The Huffington Post, March 8, 2011.

http://www.huffingtonpost.com/arianna-huffington/international-womens-day-_7_b_832691.html

16 Nina Burleigh, "Arianna Huffington: A Woman on the Verge," *Time*, November 6, 1995. http://www.time.com/time/magazine/article/0,9171,983655,00.html

17 Dr. Roger Delano Hinkins, born September 24, 1934.
http://en.wikipedia.org/wiki/Roger_Delano_Hinkins

18 Francis X. Clines, "A Phoenix on the Right Rises," *New York Times*, July 17, 1996, C1.

19 Todd S. Purdum with Melinda Henneberger, "Warren Beatty is Bathing in a New Kind of Spotlight," *New York Times*, September 28, 1999, A1.

20 Russ Baker, "Looking in the Shadows," *Columbia Journalism Review*, September/October 2000, 32-33.

21 Rich Connell and Robert J. Lopez, "Huffington Paid Little Income Tax," *Los Angeles Times*, August 14, 2003;
http://articles.latimes.com/2003/aug/14/local/me-ariannatax14.

22 Amy LeBailly, "Arianna Huffington Sees Stars Aligned for Obama," The Quindecim, October 29, 2008.

23 Dan McGinn, "Arianna Huffington Finds Her Niche," *Inc.*, January 29, 2011. http://www.msnbc.msn.com/id/35018305/ns/business-success_in_hard_times/

24 Erick Schonfeld, "Armstrong's Internal Memo to AOLers About the HuffPo Deal," TechCrunch, February 6, 2011.

25 Robert Scheer, "Betting on Arianna," Truthdig, February 22, 2011.

26 Chris Hedges, "Huffington's Plunder," Truthdig, February 21, 2011.

27 http://mirrorawards.syr.edu

28 Alex Pareene, "The Story That Made Arianna Huffington Hate Tim Russert," Gawker, June 18, 2008. http://gawker.com/#!5017739/the-story-that-made-arianna-huffington-hate-tim-russert

29 Maureen Orth, "Arianna's Virtual Candidate," *Vanity Fair*, November 1994.

30 Simon Dumenco, "The Award for Most Bitterly Ironic Media Award Goes to…" *Advertising Age*, June 1, 2009.

31 "Rachel Maddow, Tina Brown, Graydon Carter Salute Arianna In Mirror Awards Video," June 10, 2009;
http://www.huffingtonpost.com/2009/06/10/rachel-maddow-tina-brown_n_214523.html.

32 Mayhill Fowler, "No Surprise That Hard-Pressed Pennsylvanians Turn Bitter," The Huffington Post, April 11, 2008. http://www.huffingtonpost.com/mayhill-fowler/obama-no-surprise-that-ha_b_96188.html.

33 Mayhill Flower, "Why I Left the Huffington Post," September 2010.
http://www.mayhillfowler.com/politics/why-i-left-the-huffington-post/

[34] Jeff Bercovici, "Mayhill Fowler's Farewell From Huffpo Prompts a Hypocritical Reaction," Daily Finance, September 28, 2010. DailyFinance is an AOL money and finance site.

[35] Bill Bryson, *Shakespeare*. New York: Harper Collins, 2007.

[36] Nicholas Carson, "The AOL Way," Business Insider, February 1, 2011. http://www.businessinsider.com/the-aol-way

[37] http://www.businessinsider.com/the-aol-way#-16

[38] http://advertising.aol.com/audiences/affluents

[39] Quoted in Paul B. Farrell, "Tax the Super Rich now or face a revolution," MarketWatch, March 29, 2011.

[40] James Rainey, "On the Media: Arianna Huffington's new challenge Can she ride the Huffington Post's knack for 'curation' and 'aggregation' and her supernatural talent for networking and promotion to success as editor of all AOL content?" *Los Angeles Times*, February 9, 2011.

[41] Erik Sherman, "AOL's Brewing Conflict: Brand Versus Journalism," Bnet.com, March 23, 2011. http://www.bnet.com/blog/technology-business/aol-8217s-brewing-conflict-brand-versus-journalism/9437

[42] Arianna Huffington, "When HuffPo Met AOL," The Huffington Post, February 7, 2011.

[43] Ryan Fuller, Ethan Tussey, Michael Curtin, Joshua Green, "HuffPo Bloggers Raise Status and Pay Concerns: Responses to the AOL-Huffington Post Merger, Executive Summary, Carsey-Wolf Center Media Industries Project, May 10, 2011. http://www.carseywolf.ucsb.edu/files/miphuffpo_execsum_final_sm.pdf

[44] Nicholas Carlson, "AOL INSIDER: Here Are 12 Reasons Why The AOL-Huffington Post Merger Is Going Down In Flames (AOL)," SFGate.com, June 3, 2011.

[45] "The Battle Over Citizen Kane," The American Experience on PBS, WGBH-Boston, 2004.

[46] Mick Sinclair, San Francisco: a cultural and literary history. Northampton, MA: Interlink Books, 2004, 121.

[47] "The Press: Four on Hearst," *Time*, April 27, 1936. http://www.time.com/time/magazine/article/0,9171,770150,00.html

[48] "Guild tells HuffPo writers: 'Don't work for free.'" http://www.newsguild.org/index.php?ID=10712

[49] Bill Keller, "All the Aggregation That's Fit to Aggregate," *New York Times*, March 10, 2011.

[50] Tim Rutten, "AOL ♥ HuffPo. The loser? Journalism," *Los Angeles Times*, February 9, 2011.

[51] Mary Vinnedge, "Arianna Huffington: Pushing the Limits; How the political insider turned blogger gained courage from failure," Success, September 20, 2010.

http://www.successmagazine.com/arianna-huffington-pushing-the-limits/PARAMS/article/1184/channel/22

52 John Sellers, "Jill Abramson Won't Wage War on Arianna Huffington," The Wrap, June 3, 2011; http://www.thewrap.com/tv/column-post/jill-abramson-arianna-huffington-war.

53 Paul McDougall, "Arianna Huffington An AOL Stock Tout?" Information-Week, May 23, 2011
http://www.informationweek.com/news/internet/social_network/229625413.

54 Leena Rao, "AOL CEO Tim Armstrong: Paid Content Can Work," Tech-Crunch, May 23, 2011; http://techcrunch.com/2011/05/23/aol-ceo-tim-armstrong-paid-content-can-work/.

55 Jeff Poor, "Arianna Huffington's tip for success: 'Women should sleep their way to the top,'" The Daily Caller, June 3, 2011;
http://dailycaller.com/2011/06/03/arianna-huffingtons-tip-for-success-women-should-sleep-their-way-to-the-top/#ixzz1OLgvxFnm.

www.ingramcontent.com/pod-product-compliance
Lightning Source LLC
Chambersburg PA
CBHW051433090426
42737CB00014B/2945